THE 1980s
Maclean's Chronicles the Decade

THE 1980s

Maclean's Chronicles the Decade

Edited By
KEVIN DOYLE AND ANN JOHNSTON

PRINCIPAL PHOTOGRAPHY BY BRIAN WILLER

KEY PORTER BOOKS

CANADIAN CATALOGUING IN PUBLICATION DATA

Main entry under title:

The 1980's : Maclean's chronicles the decade

ISBN 1-55013-141-9

1.   Twentieth century.

CB428.N56   1989   909.82'8   C89-094078-9

MACLEAN'S EDITORS
Kevin Doyle and Ann Johnston
ASSISTANT EDITOR
Heather Starke

EDITOR
Jennifer Glossop
EDITORIAL ASSISTANT
Shaun Oakey
RESEARCH
Brian Bethune
Scott Gardiner

ART DIRECTION
C.P. Wilson Graphic Communication
DESIGN
Catherine Wilson
SUPPORT STAFF
Phyllis Black

PHOTO EDITOR
Natalie Pavlenko
PHOTO RESEARCH
Mary Dwyer

TYPESETTING
Compeer Typographic Services Ltd.

Printed and bound in
the United States of America

Key Porter Books Limited
70 The Esplanade
Toronto, Ontario
Canada M5E 1R2

89 90 91 92 93 5 4 3 2 1

ACKNOWLEDGMENTS

The guiding force behind this book was *Maclean's* senior editor Ann Johnston, a journalist of remarkable talent and commitment. As *Maclean's* first book, it was possible only with the unflagging support and encouragement of the publisher, James Warrilow. *Maclean's* managing editor, Robert Lewis, brought his unswerving professionalism to bear on the whole project. Assistant editor Heather Starke was a leading member of the editing and photo selection team and Marijke Leupen, *Maclean's* photo editor when the book was in its production stages, offered her enlightened advice. Chief of Information Services, Linda Bailey, co-ordinated the research and fact-checking operations. Finally, every member of the magazine's staff, at different times and in many ways, contributed to the completion of this book.

PAGE 2:
In one of the decade's most glorious spectacles, Canadian figure skater Brian Orser proudly led the country's competing athletes at the opening of the 1988 Winter Olympics in Calgary.

FOLLOWING PAGES:
Born in 1980 and outlawed in 1982, the Solidarity trade union became legitimate again late in the decade. In 1989 it won a decisive majority of the popular vote in Poland's first free elections since the Second World War, becoming a beacon of hope for millions chafing under hard-line Communist rule.

Contents

A DECADE OF REVOLUTION

Polish-born Pope John Paul II, on his third official visit to his homeland in 1987, stood in sombre profile with General Wojciech Jaruzelski, head of a regime that finally recognized — uneasily — the Roman Catholic Church.

AFTER JOHN BAYNE MACLEAN BOUGHT *BUSINESS: THE Business Man's Magazine* in 1905, changing its name to *The Busy Man's Magazine* in December of that year and finally, in a spurt of self-confidence, to *Maclean's* in July, 1911, he talked of creating a weekly magazine of news. There were some delays. But in 1978, following the dream of Editor Peter C. Newman and nourished by the publishing genius of Lloyd Hodgkinson, the weekly *Maclean's* appeared on the scene and went on to chronicle the hopes and fears, dreams and deceptions that shaped the 1980s.

With its own bureaus from Vancouver to Halifax and Washington to Moscow, *Maclean's* charted the Reagan Revolution as it blazed across America, documented Margaret Thatcher's efforts to bury Britain's postwar socialism, and covered the historic Free Trade Agreement between Canada and the United States. The magazine's staff also described, analyzed and photographed the end of a chapter of history known as the Cold War. That explosive conflict reached both an extreme and a resolution in the Eighties: at the beginning of the decade, Ronald Reagan echoed the spirit of earlier times when he described the Soviet Union as an "evil empire"; in 1988, Reagan and Mikhail Gorbachev strolled through Red Square like a couple of Tammany politicians, pleased with themselves, and each other, and straining to shake every outstretched hand.

It was, indeed, an age of revolution, unprecedented in its extent, except during periods of outright war. For the most part, the revolutions were started by people whose freedoms had been trampled for decades or longer. In the Philippines, a popular uprising exploded into a nationwide protest that forced strongman Ferdinand Marcos into exile and placed Corazon Aquino in power. In Pakistan, years of repression ended when authoritarian President Zia ul-Haq was killed in a plane crash and waves of popular support swept Benazir Bhutto into office. Under Mikhail Gorbachev, the Soviet Union underwent a more managed revolution, but in that country's Baltic republics the pressures for independence threatened to break the bonds of peaceful protest. In South Korea, mass protests forced the resignation of Chun Doo-hwan and the election of Roh Tae-woo. And in China, the most breathtaking revolt of all ended the decade. Millions of students led working people in vast demonstrations calling for greater freedom, before the country's elderly leaders carried out a brutal repression. But the seeds of liberty

had been sown and Communism's iron grip would likely be shaken loose again and again.

Everywhere, it was a decade of wild contrasts, a time when yuppies mushroomed, young children in Iran and Iraq slaughtered each other in war, and the Pope prayed in prison with the assailant who shot him in 1981 in St. Peter's Square. A kaleidoscope of lasting images freeze-frames the Eighties. They were not all tragic or serious; some, indeed, were positively inspiring. There was Terry Fox's tortured limp, and Katarina Witt's sexy salute after skating to victory in the Calgary Games. Meanwhile, Rick Hansen caught the world's imagination with his wheelchair odyssey. Some images and events were simply fun: Madonna was outrageous; Bruce Springsteen gave a new meaning to hysteria; Jim and Tammy Bakker gave religion a bad name, and the punk look gave most people bad dreams. Joggers shared space with couch potatoes, and shoulder pads were almost as popular as Cabbage Patch Kids.

The picture etched in the mind of High Finance will likely be that of Michael Milken, the highest of the high rollers, who created a gold rush on Wall Street—and then was charged with racketeering and insider trading. There was tragedy, too: the image of a burning nuclear plant at Chernobyl; a TWA pilot staring from a window of his hijacked airliner in Beirut, and the bombed U.S. Marines headquarters in the same city.

This book sets out to illustrate in a lasting and memorable way those historic trends and momentous happenings that emerged in the critical years of the Age of Revolution and changed our lives forever. Members of the *Maclean's* staff, including bureau chiefs in Canada and around the world, as well as senior writers in Toronto, wrote the essays on the decade's major events, many of which they had reported on as they happened. In all, the editing team assembled more than 10,000 photos, narrowing down the final selection to just over 400.

As the millennium approaches, the Eighties may well be the decade that defines the twentieth century. It was a decade that was both mean and healing, a time of such profound change that it could not be imagined—only recorded. It is, certainly, a time to remember.

—KEVIN DOYLE, Editor, *Maclean's*

ABOVE LEFT:
In a historic debate in 1988, Liberal Leader John Turner and Prime Minister Brian Mulroney battled over free trade.

ABOVE:
Mikhail Gorbachev took New York City by storm in December, 1988. In a masterful address to the United Nations, the Soviet leader announced a 20-per-cent reduction in his country's conventional forces. President Ronald Reagan, posing above with Gorbachev and Vice President George Bush, described the visit as "happy and historic."

IMAGES OF THE 1980s

ABOVE:
Archbishop Desmond Tutu, the unofficial voice of South Africa's black majority, won the Nobel Peace Prize in 1984. "As long as some of God's children are not free," he said, "none of God's children will be free."

RIGHT:
In 1982 Prime Minister Pierre Trudeau and Queen Elizabeth II signed the document that patriated the Constitution. "After fifty years of discussion," said Trudeau, "we have finally decided to retrieve what is properly ours."

Millions watched in horror and disbelief as the U.S. space shuttle *Challenger* exploded seventy-three seconds after lift-off in 1986, killing all seven crew members — a tragic reminder of man's fallibility.

OPPOSITE:
Lieutenant-Colonel Oliver North became an instant folk hero during the congressional hearings into the Iran-contra scandal in 1987. North testified that he believed he had President Ronald Reagan's approval to divert Iran arms sales proceeds to the Nicaraguan contra rebels. But by 1989, when a jury found him guilty, North was merely a convicted felon.

ABOVE:
After 123 years of inactivity, Washington State's Mount St. Helens erupted in 1980, exploding with a force 2,500 times greater than the Hiroshima A-bomb. The blast flattened forests, blocked highways and sent a grey haze of ash over the northern states and southern Canada.

LEFT:
On January 20, 1981, fifty-two American hostages arrived home after 444 days as pawns in revolutionary Iran's campaign to humiliate America, the "Great Satan."

OPPOSITE:
Despite divisions within their ranks, Afghanistan's Mujahedeen guerrillas joined forces to battle Soviet troops that occupied their country for nine years.

ABOVE:
British troops recaptured the Falkland Islands in June, 1982, after the Argentines held it for seventy-four days. But the battle for Britain's South Atlantic colony cost 1,008 lives.

LEFT:
The chador and the Kalashnikov — marks of Iranian womanhood in the 1980s and of a nation in turmoil.

Less than three months after he took office in 1981, President Ronald Reagan narrowly escaped assassination when he was wounded by one of six .22-calibre bullets fired by John Hinckley Jr. The severely disturbed Hinckley had tried to capture the attention and affection of actress Jodie Foster by shooting Reagan as he left a Washington hotel.

Determined to discard her frothy image, the former star of *The Sonny and Cher Comedy Hour* surprised moviegoers with her performances in *Silkwood* and *Mask.* By the end of the decade, Cher was Hollywood's darling, winner of the 1988 Oscar for best actress for her role as a not-so-merry widow in *Moonstruck.*

BELOW:
In 1982 E. T. phoned home — and made millions of friends on Earth. He also made Steven Spielberg the richest director in Hollywood: *E.T. The Extra-Terrestrial* became the top-grossing film of all time.

TOP:
At the 1988 Seoul Olympics, Canada's Ben Johnson sprinted to glory when he beat archrival Carl Lewis in the 100-metre dash. Three days later, officials revealed that the gold-medallist had failed his drug test, and fans lost a hero — as well as their innocence.

BOTTOM:
After Edmonton traded him to the Los Angeles Kings in August, 1988, hockey superstar Wayne Gretzky wiped away tears as he discussed his departure from the Oilers, the team he led to four Stanley Cup victories in the Eighties.

Of all the rock stars in the 1980s, Bruce Springsteen stood alone as a musician of heroic proportions. His hard-hitting songs about people travelling life's highway of dreams had universal appeal. And his concerts, marathons of rock 'n' roll, were legendary. A working-class hero with high principles, the Boss was larger than life.

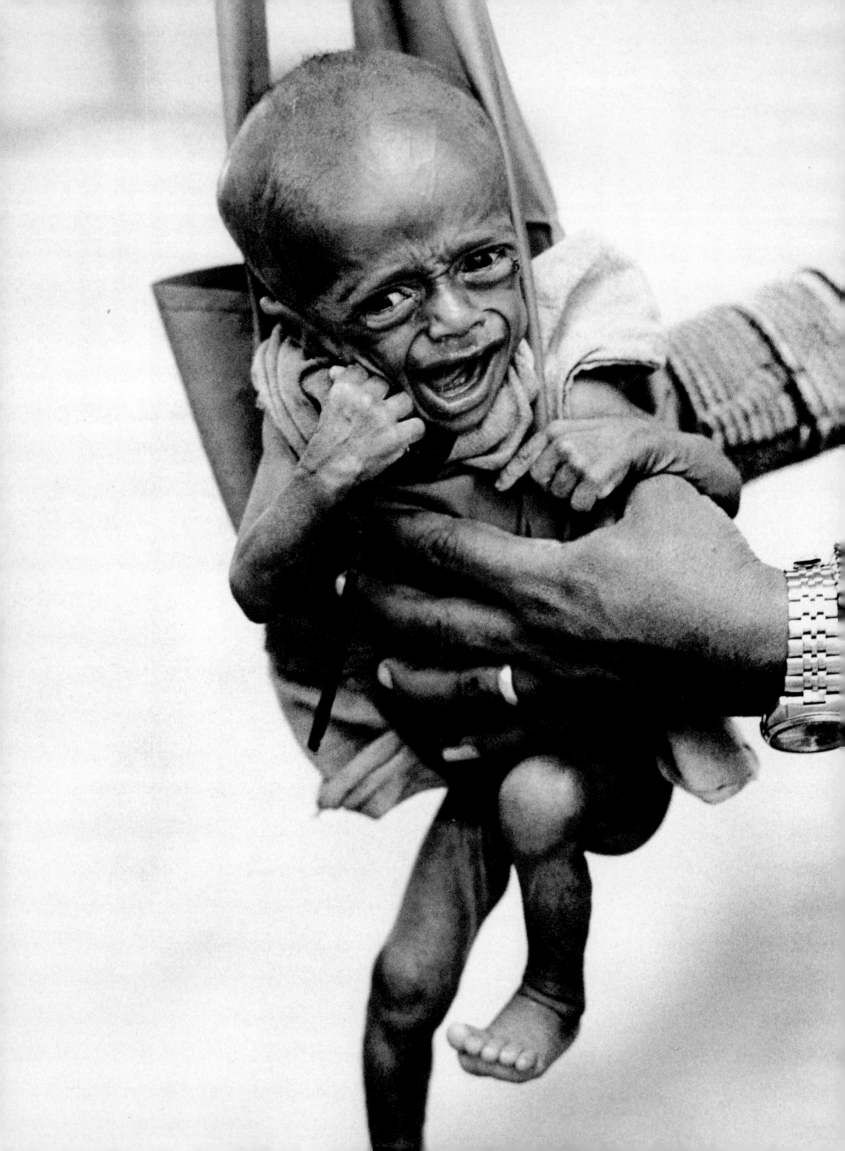

OPPOSITE:
Famine struck Ethiopia and the Sudan on a massive scale throughout the decade. Six months old, this baby weighed five pounds and was incapable of taking nourishment. He died forty-eight hours after the photograph was taken. The heart-wrenching images of hunger and suffering pricked the conscience of Irish rocker Bob Geldof, organizer of Live Aid, the 1985 benefit concert that raised more than $80 million for African famine relief. Said Geldof: "If we don't do something, then we're participants in a vast human crime."

ABOVE:
In 1987 wheelchair athlete Rick Hansen completed his incredible journey after travelling more than 24,000 miles through thirty-four countries around the world to raise money for spinal cord research. During that time, Hansen wheeled through a flood, had 100 flat tires and wheeled up the Great Wall of China.

Terry Fox, who lost his right leg to cancer and ultimately died of the disease in 1981, never completed his Marathon of Hope, a cross-country trek to raise money for cancer research. Yet the twenty-two-year-old's perseverance and courage made him an unforgettable hero.

ABOVE:
Bombings and death continued to be a way of life in Northern Ireland as the second decade of the most recent civil strife came to an end.

RIGHT:
Beijing's Bloody Sunday, June 4, 1989, shocked the world. Seven weeks of pro-democracy agitation culminated in the unthinkable when the People's Liberation Army massacred countless civilians.

OPPOSITE:
The most beguiling skater of the decade, East German beauty Katarina Witt won three world titles and two Olympic gold medals. And, with her sexy appeal, she warmed up the arenas. Said Witt: ''Every man prefers looking at a well-shaped woman rather than one who has the shape of a rubber ball.''

OPPOSITE:
It was one of the worst industrial accidents in history. More than 2,500 people died and hundreds of thousands suffered lasting damage after deadly gas leaked from a Union Carbide plant in Bhopal, India, in 1984.

ABOVE:
It was a twentieth-century nightmare, the worst nuclear disaster in history. On April 26, 1986, an explosion at the Chernobyl nuclear power station in the Soviet Union triggered a huge radiation-releasing fire that killed more than thirty people and dangerously exposed more than 100,000 Soviet citizens. Dr. Robert Gale, a U.S. specialist in bone-marrow transplants, flew to the Soviet Union to aid victims, including the man above.

LEFT:
A modern-day saint, Mother Teresa continued her mission throughout the decade. The Nobel Prize-winner rescued orphans trapped in Beirut in 1982, helped starving Ethiopians in 1984 and comforted civil war victims in the Sudan in 1986.

HEADLINES

RIGHT:
In Canada, the second half of the decade belonged to Brian Mulroney, who, with his wife, Mila, celebrated his election as leader of the federal Conservatives in June, 1983. His Tories went on to defeat soundly their opponents in the 1984 and 1988 elections.

OPPOSITE ABOVE:
She was the face of the people's revolution — and one of the most charismatic leaders of the decade. Filipinos, chanting ''Cory,'' took to the streets to bring Corazon Aquino to power in 1986, after Ferdinand Marcos — who had ruled the country for twenty years — was accused of rigging elections and was forced to leave.

OPPOSITE BELOW:
For Iran and Iraq, the start of the decade marked the beginning of a brutal and bloody war that took hundreds of thousands of lives and exhausted both nations before a truce was reached in 1988.

FOLLOWING PAGES:
In five dramatic meetings, President Ronald Reagan and Soviet leader Mikhail Gorbachev helped thaw the decades-old Cold War.

THE OUTBREAK OF PEACE

Soviet pressure forced the Vietnamese to begin withdrawing from Cambodia following a ten-year guerrilla war.

OPPOSITE ABOVE:
After years of conflict, Soviet troops pulled out of Afghanistan in 1988.

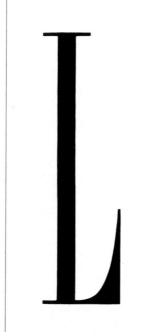

IKE A WINDBLOWN MUSHROOM CLOUD, THE DREAD OF doomsday spread across the world. Overkill, megadeath, mutual assured destruction—the phrases alone were the stuff of nuclear nightmares, and in the first ominous years of the 1980s, there were countless potential flash points. Soviet tanks rumbled across Afghanistan. Iraqi troops invaded Iran. An ex-Hollywood actor became president of the United States, and the lines he recited set off Russians-are-coming alarm bells. Could Armageddon be far behind? Could we afford to find out? So asked European and North American demonstrators, who, sporting skeleton heads and gas masks, demanded a nuclear freeze. Meanwhile, millions tuned in to a made-for-TV vision of annihilation called *The Day After.*

And then everything changed. By the end of the decade, Soviet troops had left Afghanistan in all-but-admitted defeat. Iran and Iraq had ended their own seemingly endless war, and a host of other regional conflicts had wound down as well. But most stunning of all was the abrupt about-face in U.S.–Soviet relations. After three Soviet leaders were buried beside the Kremlin wall in little more than two years, the Politburo finally sent forth a young, energetic, charismatic leader named Mikhail Gorbachev. And, less than three years later, Gorbachev and Ronald Reagan, the man who had called the Soviet Union an "evil empire," signed a historic arms accord, causing some analysts to declare—tentatively —that the Cold War was over.

The end of the Eighties presented a stark contrast to its beginning. The Red Army's lightning strike into Afghanistan, which actually took place in late December, 1979, plunged the Cold War into its deepest chill in years. President Jimmy Carter imposed economic sanctions against the Soviet Union and boycotted the 1980 Summer Olympics in Moscow. The defiant strikes of Lech Walesa's Solidarity labor union raised fears that the Soviets would invade Poland as well. And, in another dangerous international development, the Iraqis made their bold September grab for Iran's oilfields.

The Reagan era, which officially began on January 21, 1981, seemed to promise an even more terrifying confrontation with Moscow. The former silver-screen cowboy had whipped Carter with a pledge to make America sit tall in the saddle again, and to his critics at least, Reagan quickly proved himself to be a trigger-happy hombre. He ordered up a dizzying array of exotic new weapons, including research and development on the Strategic Defense Initiative, also known as Star Wars. He accused the Kremlin and Nicaragua's Sandinista government of fomenting revolution in El Salvador, and he approved the CIA's creation of a force of contra rebels whose goal was to overthrow the Managua regime. He even sent 1,900 U.S. Marines to topple the Marxist government of the tiny Caribbean island of Grenada. And he categorically rejected the grassroots movement for a mutual, U.S.-Soviet freeze on nuclear arsenals — and proceeded with NATO deployments of Pershing 2 and cruise missiles on European soil.

When the change came, it was Gorbachev who led the way. Reagan rose to the Soviet's challenge, proving himself to be more realist than Red-baiter, with a keen sense of the theatrical and of his own place in history. But it was Gorbachev, coming to power in March, 1985, after the deaths of Leonid Brezhnev, Yuri Andropov and Konstantin Chernenko, who had a mission: to overhaul the Soviets' stagnant economy, in part by diverting money and manpower from the all-consuming arms race.

The result was a four-year arms-control drama highlighted by a series of extraordinary personal encounters. After their first summit in Geneva in 1985, Reagan and Gorbachev met again in Reykjavik, Iceland, in October, 1986. There, glacial discussions suddenly broke into a flood of proposals for broad nuclear arms cuts. But the meeting ended in failure when Reagan refused to trade away Star Wars. For a time the differences seemed irreconcilable. But gradually the two sides settled on a more limited objective, and in December, 1987, on Gorbachev's first visit to Washington, they agreed to abolish an entire class of medium-range nuclear missiles — the first accord ever on the destruction of existing stocks of nuclear arms. At the same time, Gorbymania gripped the American capital, a phenomenon that peaked when the PR-conscious Soviet leader suddenly leaped from his limousine and began glad-handing the astonished crowd as though he were running for office.

It would have been unimaginable for Brezhnev or Khrushchev to have done such a thing. At the start of the decade, it would have been even more difficult to envision Reagan's reciprocal visit to Moscow in June, 1988, when the old-line anti-Communist strolled grinning through Red Square. Style had become substance, or, at least, it made us all feel better.

Along the way, Gorbachev's peace offensive also led to the Soviet withdrawal from the Afghan quagmire and to the Vietnamese pulling out of Cambodia. Other conflicts were also concluding. A UN peacekeeping force, including a large contingent of Canadians, monitored the bitter 1988 truce between Iran and Iraq.

There was no telling, of course, whether the global peace pattern was a lasting trend or merely a passing phase. Nor was there any guarantee that some unexpected event—Gorbachev losing his grip on power, a breakdown in talks on reducing long-range nuclear arsenals—would not lead to a renewed Cold War. Anyone looking back on the dramatically shifting 1980s should be wary of trying, with any sense of certainty, to foresee the future.   — BOB LEVIN

On October 25, 1981, more than 50,000 protesters participated in a peace march in Paris, crusading for a nuclear-free Europe.

IN SEARCH OF SHELTER

In 1987, 174 East Indians disembarked from a freighter at Charlesville, Nova Scotia, claiming refugee status. The ensuing emotional debate drew attention to flaws in the country's immigration process, as some Canadians protested what they said was "queue-jumping."

BELOW RIGHT:
In August, 1986, Newfoundland fishermen found 155 Tamils, natives of Sri Lanka, adrift in the Atlantic. They claimed they had begun the voyage in Southern India, but later it was learned that they had paid a German freighter captain $500,000 to spirit them out of West Germany. With special interim work permits, the Tamils settled in Canada — but their long-term status remained in doubt.

OPPOSITE:
Cambodian refugees, victims of famine and years of continuous warfare, fled when the Vietnamese invaded their country. Many lived miserably in crowded, makeshift camps inside Cambodia's northwestern border or in neighboring Thailand.

A STATE OF EMERGENCY

Nobel Prize-winner Archbishop Desmond Tutu relished his role as a major opponent of apartheid. Too potent a figure to be jailed or muzzled, he campaigned tirelessly for sanctions aimed at ending white supremacy.

APARTHEID NEVER LOOKED MORE BRUTAL THAN IT DID in the 1980s. South Africa's state of emergency, first declared in 1985 in response to widespread black rioting, brought in its wake a period of jackbooted repression exceptional even in that country. More than 2,500 non-whites were killed by the security forces, ten times that number—including many children—were detained without trial, and press censorship became progressively stricter. To a watching world it seemed that the few remaining lights were being extinguished in a government already notorious for its denial of civil and economic rights to the country's overwhelming black majority. Yet, obscured by the bloodshed and anguish, and largely unnoticed abroad, a modest program of official reform coexisted with the state of emergency. And, by decade's end, reform was the rallying cry of the ruling National Party, holding forth promise—however faint — that after more than forty unbroken years of white supremacist rule, South Africa might be moving toward something better.

That did not mean, as the 1980s ended, that one-person-one-vote democracy was on the horizon for South Africa's 26 million voteless blacks. The country remained a racist state in which the blacks, and to a lesser extent the Indians and mixed-race "coloreds," were still cruelly disadvantaged. But the fanatical belief, once sanctioned by the Dutch Reformed Church, that the Almighty *willed* such oppression had been supplanted in governing circles by more pragmatic considerations. And many observers felt that the process of reform, however limited at first, might prove irreversible.

Paradoxically, the first of apartheid's cornerstones was removed by the man who seemed to be the very personification of South Africa's institutionalized racism—President P. W. Botha, otherwise known as "the great crocodile." In 1979, a year after becoming party leader, he legalized black trade unions. In 1981, he moved to give separate and decidedly unequal parliamentary representation to the country's 2.5 million coloreds and 900,000 Indians. Even those minimal concessions were too much for the die-hard wing of the National Party, which, seeking a return to full-blooded apartheid, broke away to form the Conservative Party in 1982.

With the hard-liners out of the party, Botha got rid of other laws on which the whole edifice of apartheid was based. In 1985 his government repealed the Immorality Act and the Mixed Marriages Act, which forbade marriage and sexual relations across racial lines. The following

year, they did away with the Pass Laws, which required every black to produce an identity card on demand or go to jail. But while those reforms were being enacted, to cries of outrage from the far right, the impoverished black townships began to boil over with demands for more fundamental change. Rioting, school boycotts, police brutality and conflict within the black community between supporters and opponents of the outlawed African National Congress culminated in a state of emergency and brought Botha's cautious reform program to a halt.

Overseas, the impact was dramatic. Public demands for effective economic action against the apartheid regime rose to a new pitch, particularly in the United States and in Canada, where the newly elected Progressive Conservative government was quick to respond. Seeking to take a leadership role within the Commonwealth on the issue, Prime Minister Brian Mulroney announced a tightening of trade sanctions and promised the UN General Assembly that Canada would take even stronger measures — possibly including a

break in diplomatic relations — if Pretoria did not improve its deplorable human rights record. But the sanctions proved ineffective — trade between the two countries increased markedly in 1988 — and Mulroney never did make good on his threat to sever ties.

Still, South Africa could not remain impervious to world opinion, or to the long-term consequences of sanctions. With a surface calm restored to the townships, Pretoria sought to improve its image if not its behavior. In response to U.S. pressure, it entered into negotiations with Marxist Angola and its Cuban allies and eventually agreed to a regional peace plan under which Cuban forces withdrew from Angola in return for a South African withdrawal from Namibia. And at home the stalled reform process stirred to life again, stimulated by Botha's retirement as party leader in February, 1989, and his replacement by the younger, more pragmatic F. W. de Klerk, who promptly declared his commitment to "a totally new South Africa."

Black leaders were skeptical. Nobel Prize winner Archbishop Desmond Tutu, widely considered the unofficial voice of the country's black majority, dismissed de Klerk's pledge as a hoax. And, indeed, whatever his true intentions, de Klerk had to move cautiously. In the 1987 elections, the Conservatives had done well, winning 26.8 per cent of the white vote to the National Party's 52.7 per cent, supplanting the white liberal Progressive Federal Party as the official opposition. The Conservatives also made gains in the 1988 municipal elections, reflecting growing hard-line opposition to the erosion of apartheid.

As the decade, and the century, drew to a close, one key test of de Klerk's sincerity was the fate of the widely respected black nationalist leader Nelson Mandela, incarcerated since 1962 on treason charges. Despite the black community's ostracism of his wife, Winnie, Mandela remained the one man most blacks, and many whites, looked up to, and the one man with whom the Nationalists might be able to hold meaningful negotiations. Sincere or not, negotiation had become the government's watchword, and the world could only hope that the pattern would continue during the 1990s.   —JOHN BIERMAN

TOP:
Winnie Mandela lost status and disillusioned millions around the world by appearing to condone the alleged violence of her bodyguards, the "Mandela United Football Club."

ABOVE:
Mourners gathered at mass funerals, scenes of grief and defiance that were frequently interrupted by police and the army.

FOLLOWING PAGES:
South African police, wielding bull whips, subdued a 1985 Cape Town demonstration.

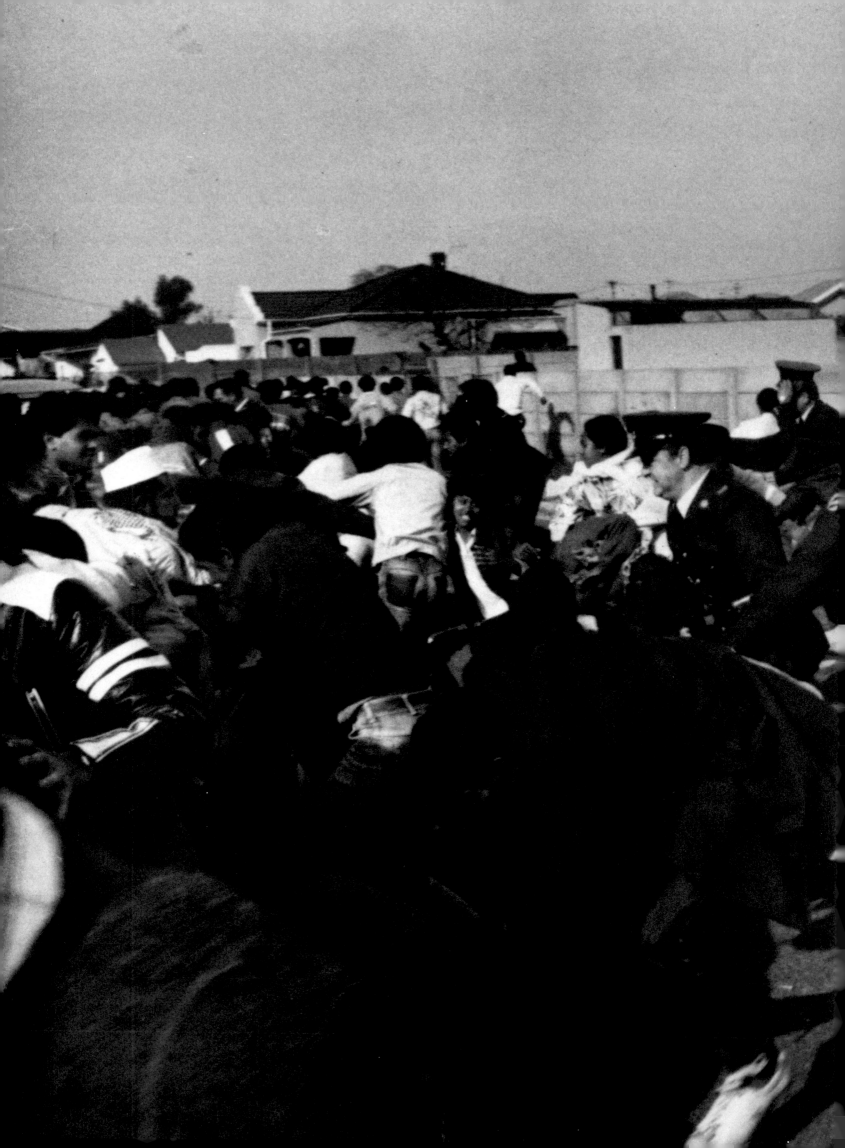

A REGION UNDER FIRE

Israeli troops carried out a policy of ''force, might and beatings.''

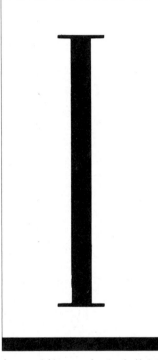

I N THE MIDDLE EAST, THE DECADE DAWNED TO A remarkable spectacle. On February 18, 1980, the Star of David was hoisted over Israel's new embassy in Cairo and three days later the Egyptian flag was raised in Tel Aviv. The opening of diplomatic relations between the Jewish state and the leading Arab nation was a first fruit of the 1978 Camp David accord—a pact that many Westerners regarded as a decisive step toward peace in one of the world's most troubled regions. But long before the decade was out, that hopeful illusion evaporated. And by the time the 1980s drew to a close, other illusions about the Middle East had faded as well.

First to go was Israel's already dented reputation as a nation that made war only in self-defence and always reluctantly—demolished by its 1982 invasion of Lebanon. Six years later, the PLO's lingering image as a terrorist organization was softened somewhat by Yasser Arafat's acknowledgment of Israel's right to exist and his renunciation of terrorism. And the world's perception of the West Bank and Gaza Strip Palestinians as a supine people willing to endure indefinite occupation was laid to rest by the *intifadeh*, or uprising, that began in December, 1987. In short, this was the decade in which the Israelis lost face and the Palestinians found backbone.

Arguably, the Israeli invasion of Lebanon might never have happened except for the Israeli-Egyptian peace treaty. With Egypt removed from the military equation, Defence Minister Ariel Sharon felt free to strike without fear of provoking a general Arab–Israeli war. At first the invasion was presented as a limited operation designed to push the PLO back sufficiently to put Israel's northern settlements out of rocket range. But Sharon's tanks and guns subjected Beirut to a prolonged bombardment. Their declared targets were the estimated 6,000 PLO fighters trapped inside the Lebanese capital with their leader, Arafat. But scores of thousands of civilians were trapped, too, and world condemnation of Israel became strident. Intensive diplomatic activity led to a ceasefire in which the PLO fighters were evacuated. But then, with the Israelis in control of Beirut, their Christian Phalangist allies moved into two Palestinian refugee camps and massacred more than 700 people, mostly women and children. International commentators condemned Israel, and an official Israeli inquiry confirmed that political and military leaders — especially Sharon—were indirectly responsible for the massacre.

Still, it seemed that the main objective of the invasion had been achieved: the PLO's military capability had been virtually smashed, its fragile unity shattered and its leader discredited. But, as so often before, Arafat managed to bounce back and reassert his supremacy within the Palestinian movement, a major factor in the PLO's faltering progress toward greater international acceptability. Just the same, it was not until the Palestinians of the occupied territories — tired of waiting for the PLO to liberate them — took matters into their own hands that Arafat began transforming acceptability into respectability by cajoling his movement into a moderate posture.

Though it had long been germinating, the beginning of the *intifadeh* can be dated precisely. It started on December 9, 1987, the day after four Palestinians were killed in a collision with an Israeli army vehicle in the Gaza Strip. Riots broke out in protest at what was widely believed to have been a deliberate act by the Israelis. And soon the rioting spread to the West Bank as the rage and frustration of twenty years of occupation spilled over. Hundreds of stone-throwing Palestinians — mostly boys and young men — were shot dead, and thousands were wounded. When even Israel's friends abroad condemned such measures, Defence Minister Yitzhak Rabin decreed instead the use of "force, might and beatings."

That did little to improve Israel's image abroad. Indeed, the almost nightly footage of Israeli soldiers beating young rioters with boots and billy clubs produced the same kind of reaction in Europe and North America as the scenes of the bombardment of Beirut had six years before. The Israeli people themselves were torn over what was being done in their name, and so were the normally supportive Jewish communities in the United States and Canada.

With the "children of the stones," as they were called, now setting the pace, and the West increasingly sympathetic toward Palestinian demands for a state of their own, the fractious PLO resolved its internal conflicts. In November, 1988, the Palestine National Council proclaimed a Palestinian ministate in the West Bank and Gaza Strip, in coexistence with Israel. That was clearly a triumph for Arafat over the PLO hard-liners, who insist on nonrecognition of Israel and the return of all pre-1948 Palestine. But it was not enough to persuade the Americans to end their boycott of the PLO, an essential prerequisite for any negotiated settlement.

Indeed, U.S. Secretary of State George Shultz refused Arafat a visa to address the United Nations in New York City, labelling him an accessory to terrorism. But a breathtaking about-face was in the offing. In Geneva on December 14, Arafat finally spoke the words that ended the U.S. boycott, affirming Israel's right to "exist in peace and security" and "totally and absolutely [renouncing] all forms of terrorism." Within three hours, Shultz announced that Washington would open contacts with the PLO. Three months later, Canada followed suit.

Although Israeli Prime Minister Yitzhak Shamir kept insisting he would never negotiate with the PLO and never permit the creation of an independent Palestine, his declarations began to sound increasingly unrealistic. Only an optimist could claim that a comprehensive Middle East peace was in sight. But the feeling persisted that an essential watershed had been crossed and that the 1990s would bring new thinking to bear from all sides on one of the world's most intractable problems. — **JOHN BIERMAN**

Young people led the Palestinian uprising, their cause symbolized by their outlawed flag.

ABOVE:
In December, 1988, a new chapter began in the long search for peace in the middle East when PLO leader Yasser Arafat laid out his organization's new philosophy of moderation. "We totally and absolutely renounce all forms of terrorism," Arafat declared. "Enough is enough."

In 1982 the world reacted in horror when hundreds of Palestinian men, women and children were slaughtered at the Sabra and Shatila refugee camps. Although Lebanese Christian Phalangists were responsible for the massacre, their allies, the Israelis, were in control of Beirut at the time. When an official inquiry later confirmed that Israeli leaders — especially Defence Minister Ariel Sharon — were indirectly responsible for the atrocity, the country suffered a major setback.

ABOVE:
As war raged in Lebanon, it brought in its wake a rash of hostage-takings by pro-Palestinian groups — and disaster for the U.S. Marines. Sent by President Ronald Reagan to try to restore peace in Beirut, the marines withdrew in 1984 shortly after 241 servicemen were killed in the suicide-bombing of their compound.

Three Americans were among a number of hostages freed through the efforts of Anglican Church envoy Terry Waite, but in 1987 Waite was himself kidnapped by Arab terrorists.

OPPOSITE:
A red Ferris wheel stood dramatically juxtaposed against Beirut, under fire during the 1982 Israeli bombardment.

ABOVE:
For the frontline troops of the *intifadeh*, stones were ammunition in their battle against Israelis occupying the West Bank. Palestinian youths attacked advancing troops until gunfire forced them to scatter.

THE IRAN-IRAQ WAR

Spouting hatred and sponsoring terrorism, Ayatollah Ruhollah Khomeini was the West's number-one enemy through most of the Eighties. Ending the Iran-Iraq war in 1988 without victory was "like taking poison," he said. And when he died the following year, few outside the Islamic world mourned.

OPPOSITE AND FOLLOWING PAGES:
The Iran-Iraq war, raging through most of the decade, left scenes of carnage and casualty tolls reminiscent of the trench warfare of 1914-1918 (*following pages*). It also reintroduced a First World War nightmare: poison gas (*opposite*). In using the chemical weapons, the Iraquis also killed hundreds of their own citizens — minority Kurds — during a 1988 gas attack on a town occupied by the Iranians.

CRUSADING FOR CHANGE

In the spring of 1989, the pro-democracy demonstrations of millions of Chinese students and workers seemed a harbinger of peaceful reform (*right*). But on June 4, that hope died when thousands of troops stormed Beijing's Tiananmen Square and killed countless civilians. One of the most indelible images of that week was a lone man holding up a column of tanks (*below*). "Why are you here?" he shouted. "My city is in chaos because of you."

ABOVE:
In June, 1987, radical South Korean students — wielding rocks and fire bombs — staged massive antigovernment street protests that forced President Chun Doo-hwan to introduce democratic reforms and eventually to relinquish power.

Nearly a decade after her father, deposed prime minister Zulfikar Ali Bhutto, was hanged, Benazir Bhutto and her Pakistan People's Party won national elections in 1988, making Bhutto the first woman ever elected to rule a modern Islamic republic. Said Bhutto: ''In the stories my father told us over and over again, good always triumphed over evil.''

HERO IN A TROUBLED TIME

Ex-actors Ronald and Nancy Reagan played to the crowd.

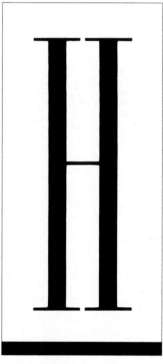

E SWEPT IN OUT OF THE WEST, A COWBOY ACTOR WITH a reassuring voice and a macho frontier message, exhorting America to stand tall in the saddle once more. Critics dismissed his economic theories and virulent anti-Communism as simplistic bromides drawn from a shoebox of yellowed newspaper clippings and from his experience negotiating contracts for the Hollywood Screen Actors Guild. But as the decade dawned, Americans were reeling from the humiliation of an ayatollah's mob holding their diplomats hostage in Tehran and Arab oil sheiks holding their economy to ransom in gas lineups at home. Against those alien forces, a country hungry for heroes turned to Ronald Wilson Reagan.

His nostalgic call to arms reminded Americans of a time when the world was a simpler place and the United States was still the toughest—and richest—kid on the global block. He read his feel-good script straight from a TelePrompTer, and when he strayed from it, his handlers—and arms control experts—often winced. But by the time he rode off into the sunset, eight years later, Reagan had restored America's good opinion of itself and, in so doing, had transformed the political landscape.

Presiding over the biggest peacetime defence buildup in U.S. history, Reagan backed his muscular rhetoric with military hardware. Still, his splurge on weaponry bore all the contradictions of the man himself: a sabre-rattling hawk who spent the Second World War not in combat, but making Air Force training films. Reagan unleashed that unprecedented U.S. firepower against tiny, unworthy targets. He dispatched 1,900 troops to storm the beaches of Marxist Grenada (population 115,000). And his covert assault against Nicaragua—with a surrogate, CIA-trained force of contra rebels—betrayed his distrust of traditional diplomacy and of a peace-minded Democratic Congress still smarting from the memory of the Vietnam War. But his can-do adventurism ended in military and political disaster, failing to overthrow the Sandinistas and rocking his own government with the 1986 Iran-contra arms scandal.

Still, the public bore Reagan no grudge. While flexing the country's military muscle abroad, he had taken the symbols of patriotism at home and applied them as a balm to the wounded national psyche. His evocations of America's greatness, repeated like some mantra to keep future shock at bay, unleashed a frenzy of flag-waving self-congratulation. Perhaps no event better symbolized the times than the 1986 rededication of the Statue of Liberty. With 200 Elvis Presley look-alikes, 850 drill team majorettes and Elizabeth Taylor swaying to the strains of ''America the Beautiful,'' Reagan reignited the statue's torch in a $10-million ceremony that bore witness to the mood afoot: upbeat, brash and unashamed of its conspicuous consumption.

Reagan's arrival in the White House had marked the coming-of-age of a new conservatism; it was not the old-style Republicanism of the country's Establishment Northeast. His followers were self-made men from the newly booming South and West, who harbored suspicions of the long, interfering arm of Washington and celebrated a raw, every-man-for-himself brand of frontier capitalism. As the White House threw open its doors to pomp and California glitz, it signalled a change not just of philosophy and style but of values. Reagan's administration winked at decades of antitrust laws and regulatory niceties, giving birth to the age of leveraged buy-outs and corporate raids. On a flood tide of junk bonds and paper profits, Wall Street hurtled giddily toward its own day of reckoning, the 1987 stock market crash known as Black Monday — an indication that even the money markets seemed to be acknowledging that greed had gone too far.

For almost seven years, the nation had been on a credit-card spree led by the White House itself. Reagan had tamed the rampant inflation and soaring unemployment he inherited. But to many that recovery seemed both false and fragile, a hollow victory achieved at a cost that could stunt the dreams of generations to come. Not only had Reagan nearly tripled the national debt; he had transformed the country from the world's number-one creditor to the number-one debtor nation. Said Jeff Faux, president of the liberal Economic Policy Institute: ''Reagan told us to stand tall in the saddle. Then he mortgaged the horse.''

While the rich had grown ostentatiously richer, the poor had grown more numerous. Between them, the gap had widened, leaving a nation increasingly polarized. An estimated three million homeless roamed the country's streets. And at the bottom of sociologists' diagrams appeared an alarming new phenomenon known as an ''underclass'' — mainly black, urban, illiterate and unemployable. Many of its members numbed their hopelessness with drugs and registered their existence in a soaring crime rate. With social and educational programs drastically pared back, their prospects were bleak. The budgetary urgency created by Reagan's deficits had changed the nature of the national debate, moving it sharply to the right. By the end of the decade, few dared to call for a boost in social spending.

TOP:
Republican George Bush and his controversial running mate, Dan Quayle, swept to a convincing victory in the 1988 election. On election night, Bush vowed, ''When I said I wanted a kinder, gentler nation, I meant it.''

ABOVE:
In 1983 U.S. troops invaded the Marxist-ruled island of Grenada.

That shift in the political compass may be the most lasting mark Reagan left on the country. As the Eighties waned, the arms treaty he negotiated with the Soviets helped put an end to the Pentagon's wish lists. And his ethic of rugged individualism gave way to George Bush's call for a kinder, gentler sense of community. But the coalition of southern and western conservatives that had come together under Reagan's banner had seen many of their values embraced as mainstream articles of faith. If America was indeed back, as Reagan's ad team boasted, its face would never again be the same. —MARCI McDONALD

It was one of the worst shooting incidents recorded in U.S. history. Before he was shot and killed by a police sharpshooter, James Huberty murdered twenty-one people and wounded nineteen others at a McDonald's restaurant in San Ysidro, California, in 1984.

RIGHT:
In January, 1989, a policeman's fatal shooting of a black motorcyclist touched off three nights of arson and looting in Miami's impoverished Overtown section. The rioting left $1 million in damages — and reminded the world of the racial strife evident elsewhere in the country.

To some he was a hero, to others, a villain. Bernhard Goetz gained international attention in 1984 after he shot four black men on a New York City subway train who, he claimed, were about to rob him. Goetz was later acquitted of attempted murder.

BELOW:
Ronald Reagan and his wife, Nancy, brought glamour — and Frank Sinatra — to the White House.

FOLLOWING PAGES:
Panamanian strongman Manuel Noriega tried to rig the nation's May, 1989, elections. But when opposition candidates appeared to win the vote, a pro-government gang brutally beat vice-presidential candidate Guillermo Ford and others, and Noriega declared the elections null and void.

For almost the entire decade, a brutal civil war raged in El Salvador as government forces opposed leftist guerrillas. Then, with a promise to talk to the rebels and end the war that had claimed the lives of tens of thousands, right-wing National Republican Alliance candidate Alfredo Cristiani — a relative novice — won the election.

In Nicaragua, eight years of civil strife between the leftist Sandinista government and U.S.-backed contra rebels claimed more than 20,000 lives and drained the national economy.

President Ronald Reagan had threatened in 1981 to take "swift and effective retribution" against terrorism. Five years later, locked in a battle of wills with Libyan strongman Colonel Moammar Gadhafi (*left*), Reagan did just that. The bombing of a West Berlin disco (*below*), frequented by GIs, in which an American soldier died and 230 other people were injured, triggered a reprisal raid by U.S. jets on Gadhafi's headquarters in Tripoli. More than 100 Libyans were killed, including Gadhafi's fifteen-month-old daughter. The Libyan leader vowed to retaliate, but stated: "We will not kill your children. We are not like you."

A NATION IN TRANSITION

Fresh from an electoral triumph that produced his second consecutive mandate on November 21, 1988, Prime Minister Brian Mulroney and his wife, Mila, hosted a visit to Ottawa by President George Bush and his wife, Barbara.

BELOW:
Prime Minister for only seventy-nine days in 1984, John Turner failed to lead his party back to power in 1988. The loss capped four stormy years for the Liberal leader, whose resignation in 1989 forced the party to search for a successor to revive Liberal fortunes.

OPPOSITE:
After eleven memorable years as Prime Minister, Pierre Elliott Trudeau was defeated by Joe Clark on the eve of the Eighties — only to be reinstated in the February, 1980, election. Four years later, after a solitary walk in a snowstorm, the enigmatic Trudeau — by turn charming or arrogant, brilliant or stubborn — announced his departure from politics.

Pierre Trudeau basked in the applause of his parliamentary colleagues on December 2, 1981, when, after fourteen months of debate, the Commons voted overwhelmingly to patriate Canada's 114-year-old Constitution from Britain.

In the early part of the decade, with the end of his nine-month tenure as Conservative prime minister and his defeat as the party leader, Joe Clark seemed to have an unshakable image as a weak politician. But with his appointment to the external affairs department in 1984, that perception changed dramatically as he earned the respect of diplomats around the world.

TOP LEFT:
Brian Mulroney and Ronald Reagan enjoyed a close relationship, sharing a rendition of ''When Irish Eyes Are Smiling'' at the 1985 ''Shamrock Summit'' in Quebec City.

TOP RIGHT:
His passionate defence of ordinary Canadians made Ed Broadbent one of the most popular political figures of the decade. Yet his New Democratic Party was never able to achieve the breakthrough it sought at the polls.

Jean Chrétien captured hearts but not votes at the 1984 Liberal leadership convention. After his loss to John Turner, Chrétien left Parliament and joined a Toronto law firm. But the former cabinet minister did not hide his leadership aspirations.

When John Turner's attack on the Canada-U.S. Free Trade Agreement struck a sympathetic chord among Canadians in 1988, Brian and Mila Mulroney stepped away from the Conservatives' carefully scripted campaign and intensified their electioneering.

THE BATTLE FOR QUEBEC

René Lévesque's death in 1987 took some of the fire from Quebec separatism.

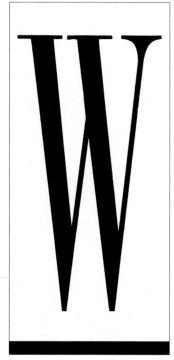

WELCOME TO THE EIGHTIES." WITH THAT ENIGMATIC opener, Pierre Elliott Trudeau, the born-again prime minister, stepped forward in a teeming Ottawa ballroom to acknowledge the cheers that greeted his return to power on February 18, 1980. The politics of the decade had begun much as they had ten years earlier: Trudeau was in Ottawa challenging Quebec nationalists for control of French language, French culture and the soul of the nation. He had once declared, "I am trying to put Quebec in its place — and the place of Quebec is in all of Canada." But now, with René Lévesque's referendum on sovereignty-association looming, Trudeau faced the ultimate test of his career-long campaign. Before the decade ended, he had won. Through the searing power of Trudeau's personality, the undeniable force of French Power in Ottawa and the support of English Canada, Quebec had been kept in Confederation.

But the price was steep. On May 20, 40.6 per cent of Quebecers voted for independence — and 100 per cent seemed to want dramatic reform of the Constitution to give Quebec more power. In the argot of the constitutional wars, Canada's fundamental law first had to be "patriated" from Westminster and then amended. But Trudeau could not persuade the provincial premiers to move, and he acted unilaterally. That triggered a dizzying round of court challenges, appeals to London and public debates. Trudeau finally prevailed. But he admitted that he had "given up the shop" to get a deal, and Lévesque, isolated and powerless to affect events, had walked out. What the other first ministers took away was an amending formula and a modified charter of rights. But the cost of the deal was a so-called notwithstanding clause that would allow the provinces — and Parliament — to opt out of certain charter provisions.

The nation had its constitutional reform but it also had become one of the most decentralized in the world, devolving even more power to ten provinces and their leaders, who often acted more like warlords than statesmen. At the end of the decade, the decentralizing continued under Prime Minister Brian Mulroney and a new generation of premiers who plunged into Meech Lake and persuaded Quebec to jump in after the province received special status.

The eve of the decade had dawned quietly enough, with Conservative Prime Minister Joe Clark declaring that his "modest purpose will be to take note of some of the good ideas which have grown up outside Ottawa." First, Newfoundland won control over offshore oil. Then,

The Supreme Court of Canada's 1988 decision to strike down a section of Bill 101, which banned the use of languages other than French from commercial signs, fuelled Quebec's long-standing language controversy. Supporters of the bill scaled the seventy-foot cross on Montreal's Mount Royal to hang their banner.

Alberta became a partner with Ottawa in setting the domestic price of oil and gas. But in December, 1979, Clark's minority government emerged as the gang that couldn't count straight, losing a budget vote—and the election in the winter of 1980. Claiming the spoils was Trudeau, who had announced his resignation in November, 1979, but went on to lead the Liberals to victory three months later. Ominously, Trudeau won only two of his 147 seats west of Ontario. But he was ready to fight Lévesque and the referendum. Someone else, he said privately, would have to build the Liberal party in the West.

The constitutional debates of the early 1980s provided an illuminating glimpse of two concepts of the nation. On the one hand there was Trudeau, the strong centrist, committed to national standards. On the other were the federal Tories and the new regional powers, including Newfoundland Premier Brian Peckford, who called Ottawa "an agency of the provinces."

With Trudeau's retirement in 1984 — and Liberal Robert Bourassa's defeat of the Parti Québécois in 1985 — the power of the provinces was enormous. On April 30, 1987, Mulroney and the ten premiers, including Bourassa, tentatively agreed to what became the Meech Lake accord. With the support of Liberal Leader John Turner and New Democrat Ed Broadbent, the deal recognized Quebec as a "distinct society" with a special role in protecting the French language and culture. Meech Lake also gave all the provinces new powers to control immigration, a role in the appointment of Supreme Court judges and the right to opt out of any new national, shared-cost programs.

Although the notwithstanding clause had been invoked by Saskatchewan and Quebec on previous occasions, the Bourassa government's use of the provision in defence of French language primacy in 1988 ignited a national battle. "I am the most important defender of French culture in North America," Bourassa declared as he defied a Supreme Court decision overturning the sign provisions of Bill 101, the province's French-first language and sign law. In fury, militants burned the Canadian flag in the streets of Montreal.

In English Canada, the Meech Lake accord provoked increased hostility. There were nasty suggestions that Quebec should leave the federation. A raw kind of racism surfaced during the Stanley Cup playoffs in May, 1989, when fans of the victorious Calgary Flames waved toy frogs in the faces of les Canadiens from Montreal, most of whom were English-speaking. It was difficult to escape the thought that constitutional peace had been bought at a high price. The provinces were happy to claim their new power. But somehow the once-proud nation of Expo 67 had been reduced to something less than the sum of its fractious parts. —ROBERT LEWIS

ABOVE:
His son, Ben, was tired, but David Peterson spoke fervently after his victory in 1987, renewing his commitment as premier of Ontario. Peterson emerged as a political star in 1985, having ended the Conservative dynasty that had ruled Ontario for forty-two years. On the national stage, the Liberal premier was a prominent voice during the free trade discussions.

MIDDLE:
During his ten years as premier of Newfoundland, Brian Peckford battled frequently with Ottawa over fishing, offshore oil rights and industrial development. Stepping down in 1989, he said that he no longer had "the necessary ruthlessness" for the job.

BELOW:
Controversies, including those over the handling of Expo 86 land sales and anti-abortion statements, constantly dogged political maverick Bill Vander Zalm, who became premier of British Columbia in 1986.

OPPOSITE:
The Meech Lake accord was designed to bring Quebec into the constitutional accord of 1982. But despite the support of all three federal leaders and Quebec Premier Robert Bourassa, some provinces refused to ratify the accord.

THE ROCKY ROAD TO FREE TRADE

The re-election of Brian Mulroney's government in 1988 swept Canada into a free trade arrangement with the United States.

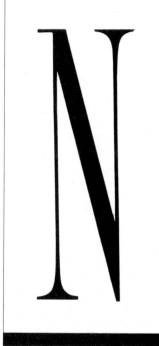

OT SINCE THE DECADE OF THE FIRST WORLD WAR HAD Canada embarked on such a radical change of direction as it did during the 1980s. And seldom in the twelve decades since Confederation had the nation been so openly riven by doubts over its future as it was during the debate over the Free Trade Agreement with the United States. Previous transitions seem in retrospect to have been less unsettling and more in step with the flow of the country's history. In the teen years of the twentieth century, Canada began to advance confidently from colony to nation after rejecting free trade with the United States and winning, largely by its war effort, the right to an international voice independent of imperial Britain's. Then, in the 1980s, a minority in a deeply divided electorate re-elected Prime Minister Brian Mulroney's Conservative government, testing Canada's carefully nurtured sovereignty in a new association with a neighbor ten times as populous and as powerful.

Free trade—with its historical echoes of playing a subordinate role in an unequal partnership—came back as a serious public policy option in the middle of the 1980s. It re-emerged as if from nowhere and, at first, it did so quietly. But, in the context of history, the transition from notion to fact came swiftly. It took Canada fifty-five years—from the first federal-provincial constitutional conference in 1927 until 1982—to formally rewrite its colonial Constitution. It took fewer than that many months, from late 1984 to January 1, 1989, for the revived idea of throwing open the world's longest undefended border—albeit guarded by cultural custom as well as by Canada Customs—to become a lawful treaty. That process coincided with other efforts by Mulroney's cabinet to diminish Ottawa's central role in the nation's life: selling off Crown corporations, opening up to foreign investment, reining in social programs, shifting power to the provinces. Critics said that such a dispersal of power posed a threat to national unity and sovereignty. But free trade, from its quiet beginnings, became virtually the only issue in the 1988 election.

The trade debate raised profound issues of patriotism. Although commercial in content, the agreement signed by Mulroney and President Ronald Reagan on January 2, 1988—and presented to their legislatures for ratification—provoked political dispute in Canada unmatched since 1911, when Liberal Prime Minister Wilfrid Laurier's similar efforts led to his defeat. Although cancellable on six months' notice, the new agreement rekindled concerns that, in the words of Laurier's Conservative successor, Robert Borden, "Canada, having once become the commercial and industrial vassal of the United States, would inevitably become the political vassal of that country and ultimately be absorbed."

Seventy-seven years later, during a nationally televised election debate, Liberal Leader John Turner reiterated Borden's warning. "I happen to believe you have sold us out," Turner told Mulroney. "With one signature of a pen you have reversed [history], thrown us into the north-south influence of the United States and will reduce us, I am sure, to a colony of the United States." Retorted Mulroney: "I believe that in my own modest way I am nation-building because I believe this benefits Canada and I love Canada." Four weeks later, on November 21, 1988, 43 per cent of Canadians awarded Mulroney a renewed parliamentary majority and, by doing so, approval to proceed with free trade.

Mulroney's own public conversion to free trade had been quicker than the electorate's. Campaigning for the Conservative leadership in June, 1983, he had ridiculed

Canadian free trade negotiator Simon Reisman (*right*) with his U.S. counterpart Peter Murphy in Ottawa in 1986.

the very idea. "Free trade with the United States is like sleeping with an elephant," he said. "If the elephant rolls over, you are a dead man." Later, Mulroney declared, "It affects Canadian sovereignty, and we will have none of it." That statement reflected the prevailing Canadian opinion since 1876, when the country's first prime minister, John A. Macdonald, enunciated his National Policy, a program of domestic industrial development designed to withstand economic and political continentalism. Although that policy was to be challenged from time to time after 1876, the first inklings of what was to bring about a firm change of direction came from another Macdonald, former Liberal cabinet minister Donald S. Macdonald, then the chairman of the Royal Commission on Economic Union and Development Prospects for Canada. On November 18, 1984, after a conference on Canada–U.S. relations in Harriman, New York, Macdonald publicly raised the idea of a free trade arrangement as a way to challenge a global trend toward protectionism. He observed that it would require "a leap of faith" on the part of Canada. In September, 1985, his commission recommended that Canadians should take that leap, stating that "there is no reason to suppose that our present confidence will be undermined by an arrangement designed only to secure a continuing exchange of goods and services with the United States."

The government, and a coalition of prominent businessmen, agreed with Macdonald's prediction. Another body of national opinion coalesced with growing vigor around a contrary opinion —notably in the cultural and academic communities, whose members voiced concerns about the overwhelming American influence, and also among organized labor and in the opposition Liberal and New Democratic parties.

On the morning after the 1988 election, Mulroney stated: "There was a view that the nation was bitterly divided over the campaign. Not so." That statement in itself formed an aptly adamant punctuation point to a dispute in which both sides insisted that truth was on their side. And in the aftermath of the treaty becoming law on New Year's Day, 1989, each side seized upon outbreaks of cross-border argument over trade issues and business takeovers as evidence that it was right. But the truth about the Free Trade Agreement, and its impact on Canada's unity and nationhood, is certain to remain elusive at least until after the treaty comes fully into effect in the 1990s —and possibly well into the next century. —CARL MOLLINS

68

ABOVE:
Prime Minister Mulroney and Dene nation president William Erasmus signed an agreement in 1988, giving the Dene and Métis 72,400 square miles of Northern Canada. It was the largest land transfer of its kind in the nation's history.

RIGHT:
Animal rights activists, who claimed that the seal hunt was barbaric, sprayed pups with dye to reduce their value. By the mid-Eighties, the harvest of seal pups had virtually disappeared, largely as a result of the outcry.

OPPOSITE:
After angry protests and road blockades, Alberta's embattled Lubicon Indians provisionally won title in 1988 to ninety-five square miles of ancestral homeland that they had sought for decades.

REINVENTING THE U.S.S.R.

After his 1988 Moscow summit with his Soviet counterpart, President Ronald Reagan announced, "My personal impression of Mr. Gorbachev is that he is a serious man, seeking serious reform."

I T WAS, ARGUABLY, THE MOST TEMPESTUOUS DECADE since the Bolshevik Revolution of 1917. When the Eighties drew to a close, the Soviet Union had repudiated much of its past and dramatically altered the path of its future. And at the centre of that revolution was Mikhail Gorbachev, a leader who seemed convinced that he could change the Soviet Union—and the world —through sheer persuasiveness. Whether chatting in the market of Kiev or glad-handing on the streets of Manhattan, Gorbachev treated the world as his stage. His audience was captivated—and at times confounded —by what he had to say. That was never more apparent than in 1988, when he delivered a landmark speech to the United Nations, promising to cut Soviet armed forces, enforce human rights guarantees and grant unprecedented support to the UN itself. At home, he exhorted his people to join him in the task of renewal. It was a bold challenge: Gorbachev's politics, characterized by the watchwords *glasnost* (openness) and *perestroika* (economic restructuring), meant nothing less than a reinvention of the Soviet Union.

At times, Gorbachev's restless vitality seemed more appreciated abroad than in the Soviet Union, where change has traditionally attracted suspicion. But his leadership marked the end of a lacklustre era: Leonid Brezhnev's "age of stagnation" and the unremarkable years of his successors, Yuri Andropov and Konstantin Chernenko. After Gorbachev took over in March, 1985, it soon became clear why former Soviet president Andrei Gromyko described him as having "a nice smile but iron teeth." To a world accustomed to dour and unbending Soviet leaders, Gorbachev combined an engaging manner with a willingness to reconsider. Gradually the Soviet Union eased its watch over other Eastern Bloc countries, pursued closer ties with many nonaligned nations and pressured the United States and other members of the North Atlantic Treaty Organization for mutual arms reductions.

The change in attitudes bore fruit in the 1988 signing of the Intermediate Nuclear Force Treaty with the United States, abolishing medium- and short-range nuclear missiles and implementing the decision to end the disastrous involvement of Soviet troops in Afghanistan. Then, Gorbachev took the unprecedented step of creating a parliament, or Congress, and threw open its membership to popular elections. Those actions captured the imagination of a world weary of Cold War: by the late 1980s, surveys showed that a wide majority of Europeans placed more trust in Gorbachev than in Ronald Reagan.

Within the Soviet Union, the new regime's record was checkered. The successes were dramatic and led to occasional speculation that the Soviet Union was westernizing its politics and economy. *Glasnost*, characterized by an often-painful reopening of the past, made it clear that very few subjects remained sacred — with the exception of Vladimir Ilyich Lenin and the current leadership. In fact, during the first session of the Congress in mid-1989, elected members subjected Gorbachev and the secret police, the KGB, to withering personal criticism. Those who had spent decades whispering in their kitchens about the atrocities under Josef Stalin now described how millions of their generation had been put to death. At the same time, an anti-*glasnost* backlash developed among people who felt self-criticism went too far. In a protest over the groundbreaking weekly magazine *Ogonyok*'s frequent revelations, one reader lamented, ''This criticism takes away my previous life, proving its uselessness, but alas, gives nothing in return.''

By the end of the decade, nationalism had become an urgent issue in the Soviet republics. Demonstrations in Yerevan, Armenia ended with the detention of 1,400 citizens in November, 1988.

New freedoms also provoked new fears and rekindled old fires. The most incendiary was ethnic nationalism, fuelled by an awareness that native Russians form only about half the population. In a country with more than a hundred nationalities spread across a territory larger than Canada and the United States, nationalist demonstrations ranging from Estonia in the west to Armenia in the south revealed the fragile allegiance of non-Russians to their state.

The same structures applied to the country's new, but limited, democracy. The March, 1989, vote allowed a rare degree of choice in candidates, but Gorbachev and ninety-nine other senior Communist Party officials sidestepped the process. They used a provision of the country's new electoral law that allowed them, as Communist Party members, to elect themselves — unchallenged — to seats reserved for the party in the new Congress of People's Deputies. But the voters instituted their own checks and balances: firebrand reformer Boris Yeltsin, who publicly rebuked the Politburo for such tactics, joined them in the new assembly with 89 per cent of the vote.

The largest opposition to change came from the growing belief that, in spite of reform efforts — or perhaps because of them — consumers faced leaner times than ever. Hasty attempts to overhaul the country's waste-ridden agricultural and supply systems succeeded only in replacing corruption with confusion. Prompted by the fear that the promise of change had often been the precursor of hardship, many consumers began stockpiling staples, which then vanished from stores. Meanwhile, state subsidies meant that average Soviets paid less than $100 a month for family housing, but six tomatoes sold for as much as $120 during the winter.

After a decade filled with both triumph and turmoil, many Soviets were concerned about their country's shattered economy and confused by the dizzying changes around them. But after four years of newfound liberties under Gorbachev, Soviet society had advanced in previously unimaginable ways. As the Soviet Union struggled to break the shackles of an oppressive past, Gorbachev's greatest achievement lay in challenging his people to challenge themselves.

—ANTHONY WILSON-SMITH

ABOVE:
Soviet President Mikhail Gorbachev and his wife, Raisa, met Chinese leader Deng Xiaoping in Beijing in May, 1989, for the first Sino-Soviet summit in thirty years. The visit added impetus to massive pro-democracy demonstrations.

RIGHT:.
Despite their personal differences, Soviet first lady Raisa Gorbachev and her U.S. counterpart, Nancy Reagan, shared a love of clothes and an abundance of style.

ABOVE:
It was to be the first in a series of public meetings. In July, 1988, more than 20,000 people gathered in L'vov, Ukraine — the second-most populous Soviet republic — to discuss national rights. But later gatherings were not as successful. The militia made its presence felt, and the meeting square was dug up — ostensibly because of construction.

LEFT:
Despite *perestroika*, queuing remained a fact of Soviet life.

POLAND'S STRUGGLE FOR FREEDOM

After eleven months in prison, Lech Walesa, leader of Poland's then-outlawed Solidarity union, let a reporter join him as he fished at his favorite stream in 1983. Solidarity, the first independent trade union in the Communist Bloc, was banned throughout most of the decade.

LEFT:
Lech Walesa received a hero's welcome in 1980 when he arrived at the Warsaw district court to present Solidarity's historic charter — a key test of the government's promise to permit the union to exist.

ABOVE:
Water cannons, tear gas and nightsticks were used to maintain order after the Polish government imposed martial law in 1981, a direct response to Solidarity's demands for freedom.

THATCHER'S CALL TO THE RIGHT

The most famous — but far from the most popular — female politician ever, British Prime Minister Margaret Thatcher carried out reforms that were among the most radical in the country's history.

WHEN MARGARET THATCHER FIRST ARRIVED AT 10 Downing Street as British prime minister on May 4, 1979, she paused on the threshold and delivered a message to her nation. "Where there is discord," she intoned, "may we bring harmony." As a wish, it was laudable, but as a prediction, it could scarcely have been more misleading. As Thatcher guided—and sometimes dragged—Britain through the 1980s, she spurned the politics of consensus. For Britons, the result was a decade of divisiveness that left most of them richer but many of them troubled by the direction their country was taking.

That new approach represented a sharp turn to the right. Of all the major Western countries, it was in Thatcher's Britain that the distinctive political and economic trends of the 1980s could be seen most starkly. By the end of the decade, the slogans of her radical conservative agenda had become the buzz words of a new Western orthodoxy. Competition, individualism, privatization: those were the concepts that Thatcher championed. By embarking on that course earlier than other leaders and by persevering where others might well have compromised, she made Britain the pioneer and exemplar of the lean, mean 1980s.

The focus of Thatcher's assault was Britain's economy. By the late 1970s, the country had slipped into a seemingly unstoppable decline, dragged down by inefficient state-owned industries that absorbed huge subsidies and were manipulated by powerful unions. Britons had seen their living standards fall far below those of other northern Europeans, and the country was increasingly impotent in world affairs. Thatcher's Conservatives set Britain on a new course. As the worldwide recession of the early 1980s gripped the country, the British government cut subsidies, slashed tax rates, sold dozens of state-run companies to the private sector and sharply curbed the unions' legal rights. The result was soaring unemployment and the worst labor unrest in decades, culminating in an epic year-long battle with the National Union of Mineworkers. In March, 1985, the once-proud union slunk back to work, divided and defeated. Britain's labor movement had been brought to heel, and British business went on to a remarkable recovery of confidence and profits.

Internationally, too, Britain assumed new confidence in the Eighties. While many in the West

RIGHT:
Homecoming for a British serviceman returning from the Falklands war.

BELOW:
Thatcher eliminated thousands of jobs in unprofitable, state-owned coal mines — but only after crushing a violent year-long strike by the National Union of Mineworkers in 1985.

still focused on the ills of their own societies, Thatcher insisted on a robust defence of Western values and a hard line against Soviet attempts to expand its influence. Those shared values forged a strong bond between Thatcher and President Ronald Reagan, restoring Britain's traditionally close alliance with the United States. But the turning point in Britain's international standing came when Argentina invaded the British-held Falkland Islands on April 2, 1982.

In a terrible miscalculation, Argentina's military rulers persuaded themselves that Britain was a has-been power without the will to fight. Instead, the country demonstrated that its martial traditions were far from dead. It dispatched a naval task force to the South Atlantic and reclaimed the islands at a cost of 255 British and 652 Argentine lives. The campaign underlined Thatcher's decisiveness, assuring her of an election victory the following year, despite grave economic problems at home.

That victory, and a third one in June, 1987, gave Thatcher an opportunity to reshape the basic dynamics of British politics. For decades, the Labour Party had relied mainly on the union movement and working-class voters, while the Conservatives drew their leadership from the traditional upper classes — what the British call the "knights of the shires." Thatcher's government attempted to break that class-based mold. It attracted workers by giving them a bigger stake in the country through sales of public housing to tenants and shares in state-owned companies to everyone. And, just as importantly, Thatcher brushed aside many old-line Tories with their inherited wealth and paternalistic attitudes in favor of a brash new breed of hard-edged Conservatives. Intent on restoring Britain's competitive position in the world, the new Conservatives had few words of sympathy for the poor and unemployed who fell by the wayside.

When Thatcher celebrated ten years in office in May, 1989, she had already been in power for more consecutive years than any British prime minister since 1827. Britain was once again respected in the world, and in the late years of the decade, it enjoyed an economic growth rate second only to Japan's in the industrialized world. And Thatcher continued to confound her enemies: the Labour Party, after a near-suicidal wrench to the far left in the early part of the decade, found it difficult to forge an attractive alternative to the Tories. Twenty-one years ago, in a speech to a Conservative party meeting, Thatcher had quoted Sophocles: "Once a woman is made equal to a man, she becomes his superior." Through skill and remarkable luck, she had indeed proven herself to be a cut above her male contemporaries. — **ANDREW PHILLIPS**

MARTYRS AND MURDERERS

TOP:
The funeral of IRA martyr Bobby Sands, who died after a sixty-six-day hunger strike in the Maze prison in 1981, followed two days of IRA-decreed mourning. A friend had said, "He knows that if he dies there will be so much anger stored up in the Irish people that it will fuel the struggle for the next ten years."

RIGHT:
Even for blood-soaked Ireland, it was a saga of unspeakable horror. On the eve of St. Patrick's Day, 1988, as 10,000 people attended the funerals of three Irish Republican Army members, a Protestant gunman burst into the Belfast crowd, killing three mourners. Days later, during a funeral procession for one of the victims, two British soldiers in civilian clothes were dragged from their car, beaten and shot dead. A Catholic priest tried in vain to revive one of them .

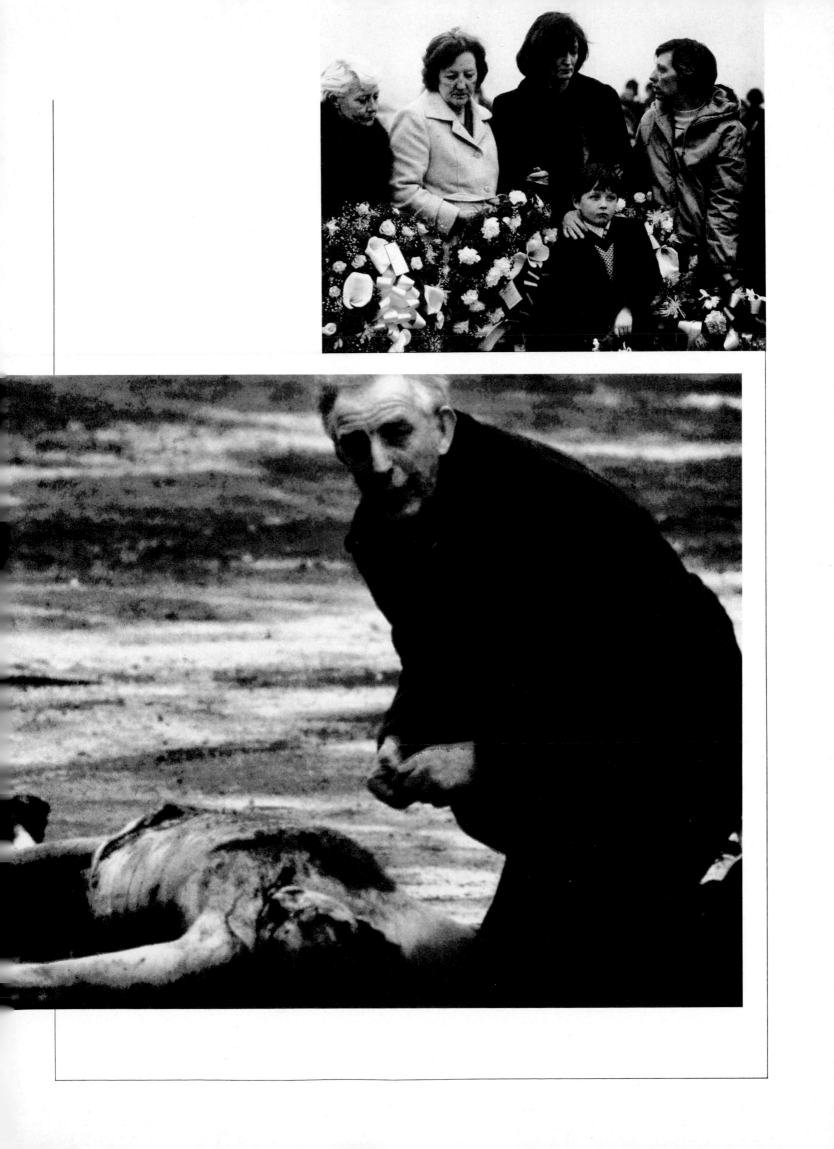

ASSASSINATIONS

ABOVE:
Rajiv Gandhi lit the funeral pyre of his mother, Indira Gandhi — slain by her Sikh bodyguards in 1984 — and succeeded her as prime minister of India. Militant Sikhs claimed that the assassination was in retaliation for an assault by government forces on extremists occupying Sikhdom's holiest shrine, the Golden Temple, in the Punjabi city of Amritsar.

RIGHT:
On December 8, 1980, John Lennon was returning from a recording session with his wife, Yoko Ono, when a deranged fan shot and killed him outside his New York City apartment. For days afterwards, thousands gathered to mourn the former Beatle, holding candlelight vigils for the visionary they felt they knew.

Hello

Goodbye

Egyptian President Anwar Sadat was slain by Islamic fundamentalists in his own armed forces as he reviewed a 1981 military parade. His assassins accused him of betraying the Arab cause by making peace with Israel and by aligning his country with the United States.

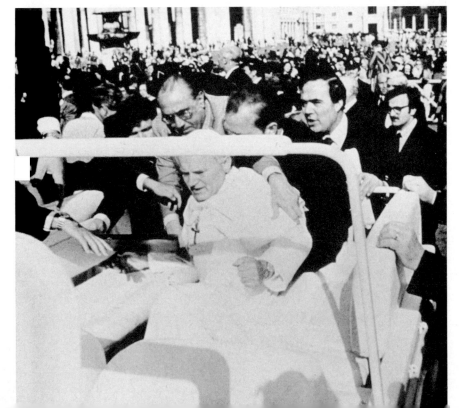

ABOVE:
The airport murder of Philippine opposition leader Benigno Aquino on his return from exile in 1983 marked the beginning of the end for President Ferdinand Marcos and his wife, Imelda. In 1986 Aquino's widow, Corazon, was sworn in as president.

A Turkish gunman, Mehmet Ali Agca, shot Pope John Paul II in 1981 as he greeted a throng in Rome's St. Peter's Square. John Paul later prayed with his assailant in his prison cell.

SCAMS AND SCANDALS

It was one of the hottest scandals of the Eighties. Former senator Gary Hart (*above*) dropped out of the race for the 1988 Democratic presidential nomination — a race that he was clearly leading — after a report that he had spent a weekend with model Donna Rice (*opposite*) at his Washington townhouse while his wife, Lee, was at home in Denver. A photograph of Rice on his lap aboard a boat named *Monkey Business* did little to help Hart's rapidly falling star.

ABOVE:
Television preacher Jimmy
Swaggart was defrocked in 1988
after he tearfully confessed to
"a moral failure" — consorting
with a prostitute. Debra Murphy
said that the minister had paid
her to pose naked in a hotel room.

Television evangelist Jim Bakker
and his wife Tammy Faye, lost
their ministry — called PTL, for
Praise the Lord — in 1987 after
the preacher admitted to having
had sex with church secretary
Jessica Hahn. Hahn later posed
for *Playboy*, the tear-stained
Tammy underwent treatment for
a seventeen-year drug addiction, and the couple made a
comeback two years later. On
his return, Jim Bakker claimed,
"I believe the devil said, "I have
to smash Jim and Tammy Bakker.""

ABOVE:
Britons were treated to a spicy scandal when former Miss India, Pamella Bordes — a parliamentary researcher and part-time call girl — was linked with a cabinet minister, several members of Parliament, two newspaper editors and a top official of a Libyan security service. None of the politicians was accused of sleeping with Bordes, but Andrew Neil, editor of *The Sunday Times*, briefly dated her. After he stopped, Bordes slashed his clothes.

LEFT:
It was a slap that reverberated across North America. Sondra Gotlieb, wife of Allan Gotlieb, Canada's ambassador to Washington, smacked Connie Connor, the embassy's social secretary, across the face. The outspoken Mrs. Gotlieb was apparently upset about a guest's late arrival for a dinner given by Prime Minister Brian Mulroney.

Charged with plundering billions of dollars from their impoverished nation, Philippine President Ferdinand Marcos and his wife, Imelda, were forced into Hawaiian exile in 1986 by a popular uprising (*below*). But they left behind an unforgettable symbol of greed: 3,000 pairs of Imelda's shoes.

The "tunagate" scandal — in which more than a million tins of rancid tuna had to be recalled — led to the resignation of Federal Fisheries Minister John Fraser in September, 1985. At one point, as Prime Minister Brian Mulroney distanced himself from the affair, Fraser insisted that Mulroney's office had known about the fish "some weeks" before the controversy became public.

RIGHT:
After winning a Pulitzer Prize for journalism in 1981, reporter Janet Cooke confessed to her editors at *The Washington Post* that her award-winning article about an eight-year-old heroin addict was largely fictitious.

BELOW:
In 1984 twenty-one-year-old Vanessa Williams, the first black Miss America, was forced to relinquish her title when pageant organizers learned that *Penthouse* magazine was about to publish sexually explicit photographs of her .

A midnight visit to a low-life
nightclub and drinks with a
stripper during a NATO trip to
Lahr, West Germany, cost
Defence Minister Robert Coates
his job in February, 1985.

A REIGN OF TERROR

For seventeen suspenseful days in 1985, Shiite hijackers of TWA Flight 847 held the world in thrall. The gunmen gradually released all passengers but thirty-nine Americans, including pilot John Testrake. The drama climaxed when the hijackers tossed their one victim onto the tarmac in Beirut. Ronald Reagan called the incident ''an attack on all Western civilization by uncivilized barbarians.''

When Palestinian terrorists hijacked the cruise ship *Achille Lauro* off the Egyptian coast in 1985, they announced there was "no shortage of passengers to kill." They shot Leon Klinghoffer, a wheelchair-bound American, whose daughters mourned (*above*). Egyptian President Hosni Mubarak, defying U.S. demands, arranged safe conduct to freedom for the terrorists in exchange for the safety of the remaining passengers. But U.S. commandos later staged a dramatic arrest, and Ronald Reagan sent a message to all terrorists: "You can run but you can't hide."

RIGHT:
Families mourned after Air India Flight 182, bound for Bombay from Toronto and Montreal, exploded and plunged into the Atlantic Ocean off the Irish coast in 1985. Investigators suspected that a terrorist bomb had been responsible for the deaths of 329 passengers and crew.

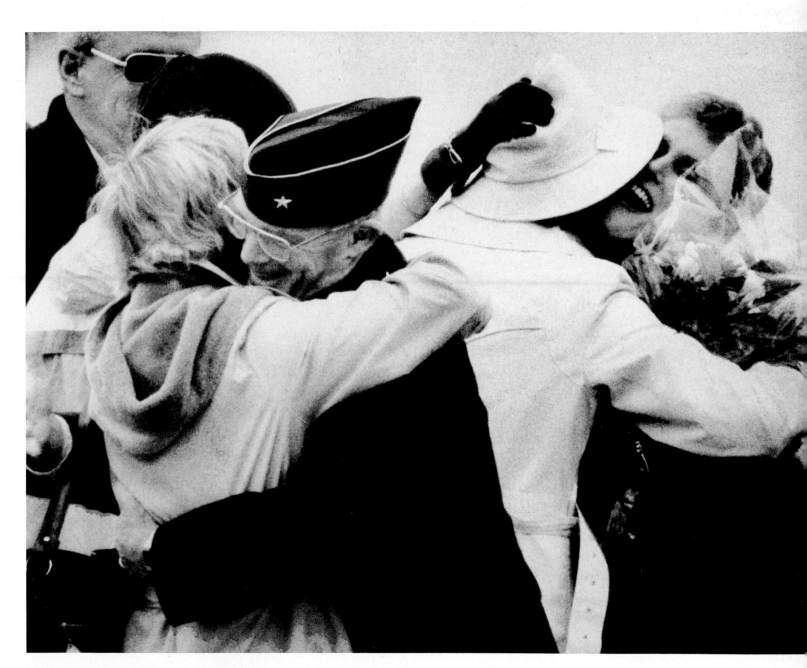

LEFT:
In 1983 police uncovered an enormous cache of arms in a small house in a suburb of Vancouver. The inhabitants — known as the Squamish Five — were convicted for the 1982 bombing of a Litton Systems plant, a manufacturer of the guidance system for the U.S. cruise missile. Several members were also convicted of the fire-bombing of three Vancouver stores selling sexually explicit videos and of blowing up a B.C. Hydro substation.

ABOVE:
U.S. Brigadier General James Dozier received an emotional welcome from his wife and relatives in January, 1982, after being held for forty-two days by Italy's Red Brigades terrorists — the group that killed former Italian Prime Minister Aldo Moro in 1978. After a dramatic raid by Italy's antiterrorist squad, Dozier was taken to a military hospital, where he requested a cheeseburger, fries and a Coke.

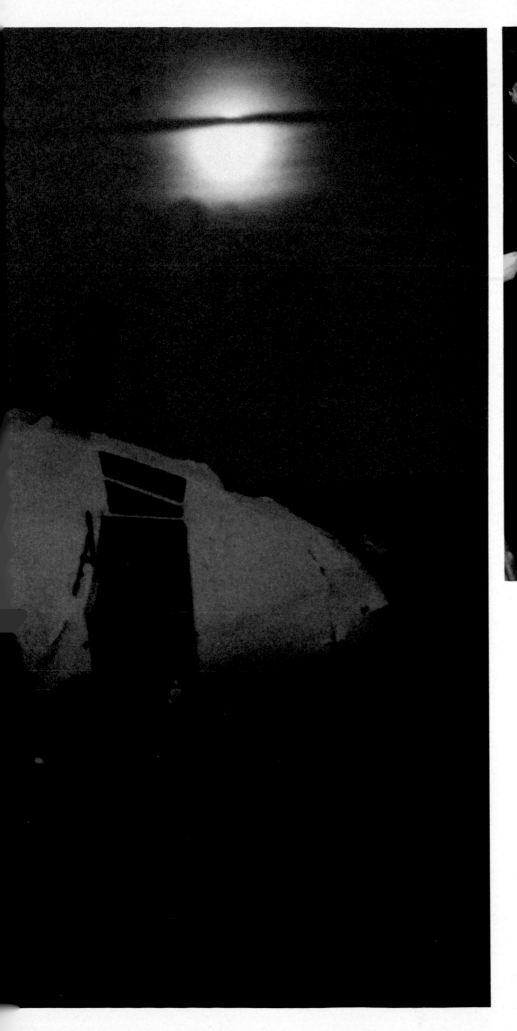

In 1988 the quiet Scottish town of Lockerbie was devastated by the wreckage of a Pan-Am 747 after the New York-bound jet exploded in midair. A terrorist bomb caused the crash, which took the lives of all 259 passengers and crew as well as eleven people on the ground. A man who had been on an earlier stage of the flight laid flowers on the grave of a fellow passenger with a note that read: "To the little girl in the red dress who lies here. Who made my flight from Frankfurt such fun. You didn't deserve this. God Bless. Chas."

TRIALS AND TRIBULATIONS

In 1981 Toronto nurse Susan Nelles was charged with murdering four of eleven babies who received overdoses of digoxin at Toronto's Hospital for Sick Children. After a forty-four-day preliminary hearing, the charges were dropped.

OPPOSITE:
In 1985 Danish-born aristocrat Claus Von Bülow clowned for renowned photographer Helmut Newton after a jury acquitted him of charges of trying to murder his wealthy wife with insulin injections. Martha (Sunny) Von Bülow had been in a coma since 1980.

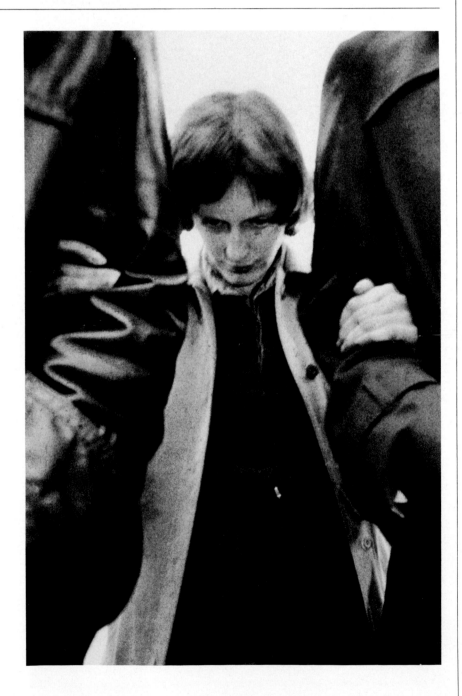

Thirty-nine years after he left France, former Gestapo boss Klaus Barbie returned under force, extradited from his Bolivian refuge in 1983. In one of the most publicized trials of the decade, the so-called Butcher of Lyons was sentenced to life in prison for torturing Jewish prisoners and sending nearly 8,000 to Nazi death camps.

OPPOSITE:
In 1988 Ernst Zundel, a Toronto graphic artist, was sentenced to nine months in jail for promoting hatred against Jews. In a pamphlet entitled ``Did Six Million Really Die?'' Zundel claimed that the Holocaust was a hoax.

104

ABOVE LEFT:

In 1983 Donald Marshall, a Cape Breton Micmac native, became the first Canadian convicted of murder to be set free after a re-examination of the evidence. At twenty-nine, Marshall had already served eleven years in prison.

ABOVE RIGHT:

It was one of the most sensational trials in U.S. history. In 1981 Jean Harris was convicted of murder for the shooting of Dr. Herman Tarnower, her former lover and the best-selling author of *The Complete Scarsdale Medical Diet*.

RIGHT:

Clifford Olson was sentenced to life imprisonment in 1982 for killing eleven young people in British Columbia. When police paid $90,000 to Olson's family in return for his cooperation in locating the bodies, Canadians responded with outrage.

After four days of deliberation, a jury found one-time Saskatchewan energy minister Colin Thatcher guilty of the savage 1983 murder of JoAnn Wilson, his ex-wife, who had been bludgeoned and shot to death in the garage of her Regina home.

BELOW:
In a tragic case of domestic abuse, New York lawyer Joel Steinberg was found guilty of first-degree manslaughter in 1989 for the beating and eventual death of his illegally adopted six-year-old daughter, Lisa. His common-law wife, Hedda Nussbaum, a former children's book editor, was also a victim of his abuse and testified against him. The sensational trial became the focal point of international alarm over domestic violence and abuse.

106

DISASTERS OF THE DECADE

In November, 1985, the long-slumbering Colombian volcano of Nevado del Ruiz exploded, triggering huge mud slides that buried villages in the valleys below and killed more than 23,000 people.

OPPOSITE:
For decades, horror and sudden death have been inextricably linked to man's attempt to command the skies. In August, 1988, as 300,000 spectators watched, three Italian jets collided at a West German air show. One jet plunged into the crowd, killing more than fifty and injuring more than 300.

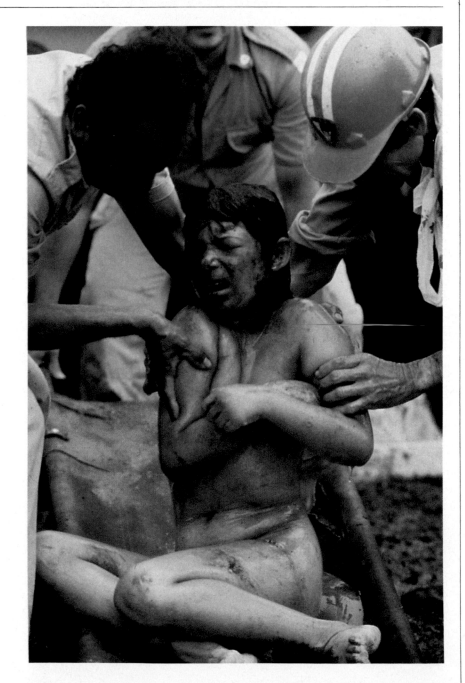

ABOVE:
United States airmen carry the coffin of one of the 248 American soldiers killed on December 12, 1985, when a DC-8 crashed moments after takeoff at Gander International Airport. The troops were on their way home for Christmas, after serving in an international peacekeeping force in the Sinai Peninsula.

RIGHT:
In 1987 a tornado with winds of up to 62 m.p.h. hit the city of Edmonton, killing twenty-seven.

LEFT:
The double earthquake that devastated the world's largest metropolis, Mexico City, in 1985 left an estimated 25,000 dead, 150,000 homeless and property damage estimated in the billions of dollars. "I drank my tears," said a woman rescued after being buried a week.

BELOW:
The earthquake that hit the Soviet republic of Armenia late in 1988 killed tens of thousands, destroyed whole cities, cut short Mikhail Gorbachev's visit to America, and — by revealing shortcomings in Soviet relief capabilities — heightened Armenian anger and nationalist sentiment.

OPPOSITE:
In 1988 catastrophic floods left 75 per cent of Bangladesh underwater and thirty million homeless.

ABOVE:
Hurricane Gilbert was the most powerful in history, leaving more than 750,000 homeless as it raged across the Caribbean, Mexico and into the United States in 1988.

LEFT:
Mourners cast flowers in memory of the 269 passengers who died on Korean Air Lines Flight 007. Moscow claimed that the plane, which was shot down by a Soviet fighter in 1983, had been spying.

ABOVE:
Like the spilled contents of a child's toy box, rail cars littered the tracks near Hinton, Alberta, after a CN Rail freight train crashed head-on into a Via Rail passenger train in 1986.

LEFT:
When part of the fuselage blew off an Aloha Airlines 737 at 24,000 feet, passengers began singing hymns. A flight attendant was killed in the 1988 accident, one of many air crash casualties of the decade.

THE ISSUES

ABOVE:
As the first celebrity known to have succumbed to the AIDS virus, Hollywood star Rock Hudson — who died in 1985 — became a symbol of courage for the thousands of people battling the deadly disease.

RIGHT:
For $13,500, New Jersey housewife Mary Beth Whitehead agreed to carry to term a baby conceived with sperm from biochemist William Stern. When Whitehead refused to give up ''Baby M,'' an emotional trial began. In 1987 the judge ruled that Stern and his wife, Elizabeth, had a right to the child.

Thousands of seabirds, otters and other animals were coated with oil after the tanker *Exxon Valdez* went aground off the Alaska coast in 1989, spilling 240,000 barrels of crude oil into one of the world's most sensitive areas of marine life. Said one naturalist, ``This spill is America's Chernobyl.''

THE DRUG CRISIS

TOP:
In 1982 U.S. automaker John De Lorean was arrested on charges of conspiring to traffic in cocaine in an attempt to save his failing auto firm. When a jury found him not guilty, De Lorean's creditors lodged claims of $100 million.

RIGHT:
When the Boston Celtics pro basketball team drafted Len Bias in 1986, the University of Maryland student celebrated with friends and wound up dead from a cocaine overdose. The tragedy sharply raised public awareness of the potency of the glamour drug of the Eighties.

John Belushi, the manic star of *National Lampoon's Animal House* and *Saturday Night Live*, died of an overdose of heroin and cocaine in 1982. Catherine Evelyn Smith, who administered the fatal dose in a bungalow at Hollywood's Château Marmont Hotel, was charged with involuntary manslaughter and three counts of furnishing and administering dangerous drugs.

He had regaled audiences with tales of his drug abuse, but comedian Richard Pryor's addiction nearly killed him. In 1980 a solvent he was using to free-base cocaine exploded. Pryor spent a month in the hospital undergoing treatment for burns to more than half his body.

A THREATENED PLANET

In the late 1980s farmers struggled to produce crops as drought scorched the earth.

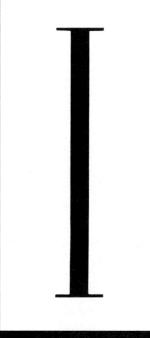

T WAS ONE OF THOSE RARE MOMENTS, A SINGLE PULSE of time after which nothing is ever quite the same. This one occurred twenty-three minutes after one o'clock on the morning of April 26, 1986. At that instant, a hydrogen fireball blew the roof off the hall housing the number four reactor at a nuclear facility on the banks of the Pripyat River, nine miles upstream from a dusty Ukrainian town called Chernobyl. The explosion hurled more than seven tons of radioactive debris into the atmosphere. It created a drifting, lethal plume that would kill more than thirty people, poison another 300, drive 100,000 from their homes and turn a thousand square miles of rich steppe into a radiating desert.

Chernobyl made the dangers of nuclear power real, in a way that hundreds of studies could not: poisoned vegetables in Italy and contaminated lamb in Poland, lakes in Sweden and milk in Brazil. At the same time, North Americans faced the heightened risk of cancer. What occurred was a kind of awakening, a realization of mankind's common destiny on a planet beginning to show dangerous signs of wear and tear. And with that particular awareness came a dawning suspicion that there might well be a limit to the punishment the planet could sustain.

It was a suspicion that unfolded with the decade, gathering strength as the evidence of impending environmental doom mounted. When the 1980s began, the ecology was the concern of a vociferous minority regarded by most as well-meaning cranks. The prevailing attitude allowed President Ronald Reagan to pretend that acid rain did not exist, permitted Prime Minister Margaret Thatcher to dismiss the environment as a ''bore,'' made it safe for Prime Minister Brian Mulroney to slash funds for environmental programs. But such blithe disregard did not halt the slow death of lakes and forests, the disappearance each year of 27 million acres of tropical rain forest, nor the annual spread of 15 million acres of desert. Thousands of species continued to face extinction, including African toads, Indonesian orangutans and humpback whales. Little was done to curb the escalating contamination of land, air and water by a witches' brew of pollutants. But in the end it was the politicians who changed their tune.

They had no choice: a series of events like the one at Chernobyl offered a glimpse of a world without a future. Leaking pesticides killed 2,500 people in Bhopal, India. A noxious tide of medical refuse closed New York City's beaches. A toxic fire cleared the Quebec town of St-

Basile-le-Grand. An American supertanker dumped 10 million gallons of oil into Alaska's Prince William Sound, one of the most biologically rich, environmentally fragile ecosystems on the face of the Earth.

It all suggested a biosphere under critical — even terminal — stress, and the point was driven home with particular force as the 1980s drew to a close. It was then that an unprecedented threat of truly global proportions materialized: scientists discovered that the ozone layer, the sheet of triple-atomed oxygen in the stratosphere that shields the globe from ultraviolet radiation, was being consumed by a tribe of manmade chemicals called chlorofluorocarbons. At certain times of the year there was a hole over the South Pole as large as the United States and as high as Mount Everest. Over a heavily populated belt of North America, Europe and the Soviet Union, ozone concentrations had declined by 3 per cent since 1969. When that startling information was disseminated, it drove people off the world's beaches, threatening to transform sun worshippers into a dying cult.

Grim as it was, ozone depletion was not the most serious atmospheric menace that surfaced in the 1980s. Far more ominous was something scientists labelled the "greenhouse effect" — a warming of the globe as a result of the buildup in the atmosphere of heat-trapping gases. Carbon dioxide was primarily responsible; mankind was the culprit, dumping five and a half billion tons of carbon into the atmosphere every year by burning coal, oil and natural gas. Scientists warned that the Earth's mean temperature could rise significantly by the middle of the next century. The implications were disturbing: it could mean the destruction of the world's food supply by scorching into near-desert the agricultural heartlands of North America and Asia. It could also complete the work that mankind had begun by finishing off whole species of plants and animals.

More frightening still was the possibility that none of this was part of a future doomsday scenario. As the 1990s loomed into view, it dawned on people that life in the greenhouse might have already commenced. The decade saw the six hottest years of the past century, part of a global warming trend that appeared to be accelerating. Hospitals from Athens to China's Yangtze Valley were filled with heatstroke victims. Forests in the South American Amazon and the North American Rockies, including much of America's Yellowstone National Park, burned. Canadian wheat farmers watched millions of acres of prime grain belt crumble into dust. In 1988, blistering temperatures and prolonged drought resulted in a U.S. harvest that, for the first time in history, fell below U.S. consumption.

People were jolted awake. Suddenly, Mulroney and Thatcher were hosting international conferences on environmental issues. Reagan's successor, George Bush, began to take acid rain seriously. Aerosol sprays, fuelled by chlorofluorocarbons, began to disappear from shelves as did foam coffee cups and nonbiodegradable plastic bags. And as public consciousness was raised, blue recycling boxes began to appear on the front lawns of a growing number of Canadian communities. It all suggested that we may finally have realized that we cannot foul our own nest with impunity. Whether that is enough to stop the erosion, however, is a life-and-death issue that remains to be resolved. —BARRY CAME

TOP:
The problem of garbage disposal reached a crisis level in many urban areas.

ABOVE:
In 1988 more than 3,000 residents of St-Basile-le-Grand, Quebec, were evacuated when a fire ignited oil contaminated by toxic chemicals.

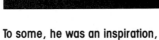

To some, he was an inspiration, to others, a baby-killer. In 1988, three weeks after the birth of his son, Dr. Henry Morgentaler won an eighteen-year legal battle when the Supreme Court of Canada struck down a law restricting women's access to abortion — sparking a storm of protests from anti-abortion activists across the country.

OPPOSITE:
Supporters of the proposed Equal Rights Amendment to the U.S. Constitution lost a ten-year battle in 1982 when it failed to win ratification by the required number of state legislatures. But they gave notice that the battle would continue. Said Eleanor Smeal, president of the National Organization for Women, which spearheaded the ERA drive: ``We have just begun to fight.''

THE AIDS EPIDEMIC

Liberace, who died of AIDS in 1987, always denied having the disease.

T FIRST, IT SEEMED TO BE NOTHING MORE THAN A CLInician's puzzle, one of an increasing number of medical mysteries that had outstripped war as a killer of mankind in the fading days of the twentieth century. During the Seventies there had been suggestions that an enigmatic malady had taken lives around the world. As more young, previously healthy homosexuals presented themselves at hospitals in 1981, it gained a name—first the derisive misnomer "the Gay Plague," and then Acquired Immune Deficiency Syndrome, or AIDS. The enigma, however, remained, and the disease gained an imposing place in the popular imagination. Unlike war, AIDS took few prisoners; it almost always killed.

By the end of the decade, the disease had become a worldwide pestilence, cutting a swath through all segments of society. In a world of heart transplants and genetic engineering, a cure was strangely elusive. And while scientists were able to identify the AIDS virus, name and number its carriers and invent palliatives, the images of those with AIDS were ultimately horrifying. Emaciated, they were often shunned by friends, family and even undertakers. All over the world they died slowly and painfully, their weakened immune systems assaulted by a series of ghoulish infections: pneumocystis carinii pneumonia, cryptococcal meningitis, Kaposi's sarcoma.

Unlike many epidemics in history, the scourge of AIDS gathered steadily in strength and virulence. By 1990 it had endured longer than the Black Death of the fourteenth century. And there were no signs that, like cholera or smallpox, AIDS was burning out. Many were inclined to seek signs of divine retribution and to lay blame. According to American fundamentalist Jerry Falwell, AIDS was "God's judgment on a society that does not live by His rule." Patrick Buchanan, a political adviser to President Ronald Reagan, also faulted homosexuality, claiming: "They have declared war on nature, and now nature is exacting an awful retribution."

As far as the media were concerned, the AIDS story had everything: sex, death, sin, mystery, paranoia, ethical dilemmas and future shock. Meanwhile, fear spread like wildfire, barely dampened by reassurances from experts. The common view was that the virus could be spread not only by contaminated bodily fluids and needles but by casual contact. Blood donors stopped giving blood; insurance companies refused to insure people at risk; TV technicians declined to film AIDS patients. Even a friendly welcome kiss was believed to be dangerous.

But behind the façade of rumor, important changes were occurring. The sexual revolution of the past two decades sputtered to a halt: with the threat of AIDS, sex could be both murder and suicide. Several singles bars became private clubs, limiting their membership to those who could provide proof they were not carriers. In 1988 Masters and Johnson, the American gurus of sexology, concluded that the virus was raging unimpeded through the heterosexual community.

Denied a cure, others reached for deeper meaning. Some environmentalists and public health experts saw it as the natural consequence of an enfeebled, overpopulated world, gathered largely in filthy cities where the virus, a new global currency, could settle at will. Said French specialist Dr. Willy Rozenbaum: "AIDS cannot be mastered in the West unless it is overcome everywhere."

Meanwhile, the very thrust and practice of medicine — a profession that had acquired unprecedented prestige in the previous eighty years — came into question. In 1988 writer Susan Sontag said that "medicine had been viewed as an age-old military campaign now nearing its final phase, leading to victory." Yet victory was nowhere in sight, and AIDS experts were speaking of a toll that would soar far higher as the millennium approached. At the Third International Conference on AIDS in Washington in 1987, a spokesman for the World Health Organization said that as many as 10 million people were likely carriers of the virus, which could lie dormant for a full ten years before emerging. In early 1989, Canada's own Federal Centre for AIDS predicted that the 2,875 recorded cases would increase fourfold in the next four years. In the past, researchers had come to terms with leprosy, syphilis, polio and, to a degree, cancer. But AIDS remained intractable, implacable, its business unfinished.

Its costs were enormous. In 1987 authorities in New York City reported a daily expenditure of $600,000 to treat the average number of AIDS patients in its hospitals. In African countries, newly awakened after centuries of colonial rule, the disease was decimating the population of young adults on whom authorities had spent much of their limited education resources. And in Europe and North America, the disease took the lives of many of the best and brightest in the performing arts.

As the Eighties ended, AIDS had become a fact of life. In fact, most city dwellers knew someone who had died of AIDS. Groups in larger cities began establishing and equipping AIDS hospices where the ill could die with a measure of peace, dignity and comfort. Discussion of the disease centred on the broad ethical issues that it raised: whether to allow the banning of young hemophiliacs from classrooms; whether to deny employment to hospital workers who carried the virus; whether to jail or quarantine sociopaths who knowingly spread AIDS; and whether to force everyone to take the test.

Societies in all parts of the world settled down for the long, hard grind of educating people about the nature of AIDS, its risks and modes of transmission, about drug use, blood supplies and "safe sex." There seemed little else to do: there was no imminent cure for the lethal virus. But ignorance about AIDS could at least be contained, and that, after nearly ten years of suffering and public trauma, was at least a beginning.

—GLEN ALLEN

ABOVE:
Controversial U.S. lawyer Roy Cohn died of AIDS-related illnesses in 1986. During the 1950s Cohn served as chief counsel to Senator Joseph McCarthy's investigations into Communist influence in the United States.

Efforts to define — and then abolish — pornography raised cries of censorship across Canada. In 1987 Justice Minister Ray Hnatyshyn proposed a sweeping antipornography law that divided the existing obscenity category into ''erotica'' and ''pornography'' — to the outrage of the artistic community. The backlash proved effective, and the bill died before the 1988 election.

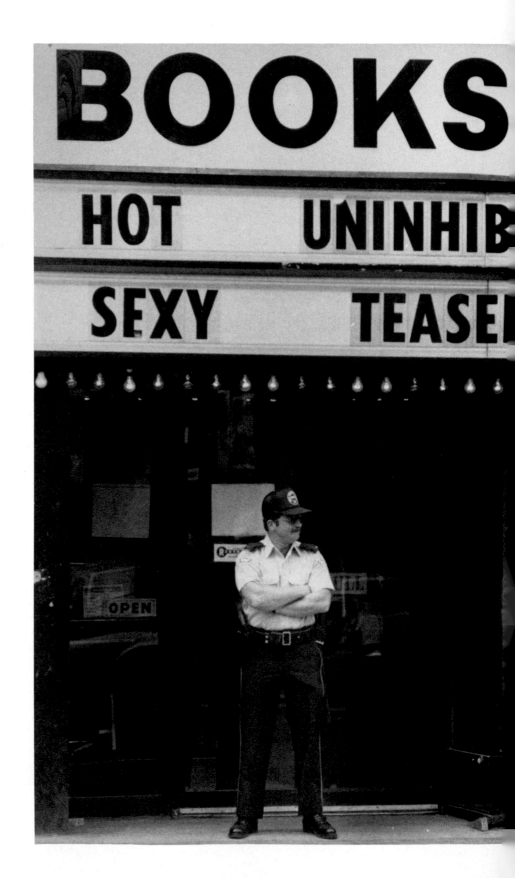

Prostitution was a growing problem across North America. As the fear of AIDS increased, and prostitutes became more aggressive, the public reacted in anger. In 1985 the Canadian government ruled that both prostitutes and their clients were liable to prosecution whenever they communicated in public for the sale or purchase of sex.

BELOW:
The House of Commons defeated an attempt to restore capital punishment in 1987, yet more than twenty-five years after Canada's last execution, the debate raged on. And in the United States, many were outraged when the 1989 execution of serial killer Ted Bundy turned into a countrywide celebration.

THE ARTS

ABOVE:
On the wide screen and the home screen, Steven Spielberg's *E.T. The Extra-Terrestrial* proved to be the ultimate mega-hit, the top-grossing film of all time.

A gifted and original artist, Michael Jackson broke records with his 1982 album *Thriller*, set new standards with his videos and performed some of the most dazzling dance sequences ever. Although his pumped-up funk dominated the airwaves, Jackson's widely reported personal obsessions — from plastic surgery to pet zoos — earned him the nickname "Wacko Jacko."

Novelist Margaret Atwood, already a major cultural force in Canada, was catapulted into literary stardom with the 1985 publication of her best-selling novel *The Handmaid's Tale* — the story of a woman living in the not-so-distant future, whose sole function is to be a surrogate reproducer.

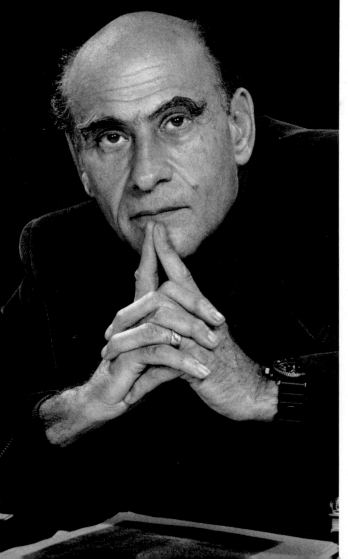

LEFT:
Canadian short story writer Alice Munro won international acclaim and a 1986 Governor General's Award for *The Progress of Love*, which examined the unease beneath the apparently placid surface of small-town life.

BELOW LEFT:
Peter C. Newman charted the history of the Hudson's Bay Co. in two epic best-sellers, *The Company of Adventurers* and *Caesars of the Wilderness*.

ABOVE RIGHT:
With such amusing, intelligent tales as *The Paper Bag Princess* and *Mortimer*, Robert Munsch became one of Canada's best-loved and best-selling children's storytellers.

RIGHT:
New York author Jay McInerney rose to the top of the literary brat pack with his first novel, *Bright Lights, Big City*, a comic and moving story of a magazine researcher hooked on cocaine and Manhattan night life.

ABOVE LEFT:
Indian-born author Salman Rushdie unleashed a torrent of Islamic fury with his 1988 novel, *The Satanic Verses*. Iran's Ayatollah Khomeini pronounced it blasphemous and sentenced Rushdie to death, offering a reward for his execution. As Rushdie went into hiding, many countries reacted with outrage.

ABOVE RIGHT:
Eminent Canadian scholar Northrop Frye published *The Great Code* in 1982, a free-wheeling study of biblical narrative and imagery.

RIGHT:
With his darkly satirical novel, *The Bonfire of the Vanities* (1987), Tom Wolfe provided a savage satire of the fast lane in New York City.

Robertson Davies, the scholarly, bearded patriarch of Canadian letters, completed his third trilogy in the 1980s. Following *The Rebel Angels* (1981) and *What's Bred in the Bone* (1985), the last of this series, *The Lyre of Orpheus* (1988), affirmed his status as a master storyteller and a literary giant.

ABOVE LEFT:
Canadian novelist Timothy Findley dealt with fascism in *Famous Last Words* (1981) and murder in *The Telling of Lies* (1986). He said that everything in his articulate, disturbing books ''hinges, turns, upon violence.''

ABOVE:
A triumphant work of art, *Love in the Time of Cholera*, by Nobel Prize-winner Gabriel García Márquez, chronicled an obsessive love that lasted more than five decades.

LEFT:
Shere Hite caused a sensation in 1976 with her study of female sexuality. But that paled beside the uproar following the 1987 publication of *The Hite Report, Women and Love: A Cultural Revolution in Progress*. Amid charges of an anti-male bias and unscientific research, the New York sociologist stood by her findings that 84 per cent of women were unsatisfied with their relationships — and 70 per cent engaged in affairs.

SOUNDS FOR A GLOBAL VILLAGE

Irish rocker Bob Geldof pricked the conscience of rock.

PREVIOUS PAGES:
Tracy Chapman, Youssou N'Dour, Sting, Joan Baez and Bruce Springsteen highlighted the 1988 Amnesty tour, an extraordinary gathering of socially conscious artists who trumpeted a human-rights message around the world.

N THE WORLD OF MUSIC, THE DECADE BEGAN ON A shaky note with the death of one of rock's true visionaries. On December 8, 1980, John Lennon was gunned down outside his New York apartment by a fan with a psychotic obsession. But Lennon lived on in his music. And his signature piece, "Imagine," in which he sang about "no need for greed or hunger/a brotherhood of man," sounded a clarion call for those he left behind. On July 13, 1985, sixty pop stars from around the world staged Live Aid, the largest charity benefit in history. With two massive concerts, performed simultaneously in London and Philadelphia, the event was global in its reach, beamed by satellite to an estimated 1.5 billion people. On that day, Marshall McLuhan's global village became a reality. Live Aid, which raised more than $250 million for African famine relief, was a mammoth rock festival for the video age. As Joan Baez told the Philadelphia audience: "Good morning, children of the 1980s. This is your Woodstock, and it's long overdue."

Live Aid was, in fact, the brainchild of Irish rocker Bob Geldof. Outraged by televised images of starving Ethiopians, Geldof organized an all-star group of British pop stars called Band Aid in 1984 to record a fund-raising single, "Do They Know It's Christmas?" That gesture resounded through the mainstream, inspiring artists in many countries to follow suit. In Canada, such national pop heroes as Bryan Adams, Anne Murray and Gordon Lightfoot recorded "Tears Are Not Enough." Of the many songs produced for African famine relief, the American offering seemed to best capture the mood of the time. With its rousing message of goodwill, "We Are the World" became a global anthem and was the fitting finale for Live Aid. Like the benefit itself, the song presented the lofty hope that rock music had the power to feed the world.

While the sight of starving African families pricked rock's social conscience, the pulsing rhythms of African music rejuvenated Western pop in the 1980s. After a decade in which disco had turned rock 'n' roll into a barren wasteland, devoid of soul, Third World music offered a new vitality. With a trail blazed by Bob Marley, the Jamaican reggae star who died in 1981, Nigeria's King Sunny Adé caused a sensation with his exotic juju sound. Echoing across the planet, Third World music cast a spell on such Western artists as The Police and Talking Heads.

That cross-pollination had its fullest flowering in Paul Simon's groundbreaking album *Graceland*, a clever synthesis of Simon's witty, urbane lyrics and the buoyant township jive and mbube

sounds of South Africa. Although the album and subsequent tour — which featured one lone white performer onstage amid a gathering of black musicians — prompted controversy, both opened the floodgates for a whole wave of African music, including the Zulu vocal group Ladysmith Black Mambazo. And in its wake, Western listeners developed a taste for a hybrid style called world-beat. A kind of pop without borders, world-beat embraced everything from flamenco pop and Hindu soul to Bulgarian folk and what one group cheekily called ''Moroccan roll.''

By the end of the 1980s, Linda Ronstadt had sung an album of mariachi music in Spanish, pop adventurer David Byrne of Talking Heads had compiled a collection of Brazilian pop, and Paul Simon had recorded with West African and Caribbean percussionists. And clearly world-beat had become a two-way street. There were as many Third World imitators of Michael Jackson and Madonna as there were Western artists borrowing ethnic sounds. Technology, as McLuhan had predicted, had taken pop to the far corners of the globe, where rap music straight out of Harlem became instantly popular in the slums of Rio de Janeiro and reggae fresh from Jamaica found a following among Australian aborigines.

In a musical convergence, global pop and humanist rock culminated in an extraordinary benefit tour for Amnesty International in 1988. Featuring Bruce Springsteen, Sting, Peter Gabriel, Tracy Chapman and Senegal's Youssou N'Dour, Human Rights Now! was the most ambitious tour of its kind ever staged. An enormous human-rights caravan, the Amnesty tour turned disparate crowds on every continent into devoted gatherings, reminiscent of communal rock festivals of the past. Each concert closed with a muscular Springsteen, a stylish Sting and a vulnerable Chapman joining the others for emotional renditions of Bob Dylan's anguished ''Chimes of Freedom'' and Marley's stirring ''Get Up, Stand Up.''

Those finales harkened back to another era when rock served as a medium for social change. Yet the image of five diverse artists, including an African superstar, performing together also underscored the new trend toward world-beat music. As the decade drew to a close, world-beat seemed to fulfil music's promise as a universal language, the perfect sound for the global village.   —NICHOLAS JENNINGS

TOP:
Mick Jagger and Tina Turner gave an electrifying performance at Live Aid, the rock concert of the decade — and a Woodstock for the video age.

ABOVE:
Paul Simon's *Graceland* infused the world with an African beat.

ABOVE:
One of the hottest Eighties talents was trumpeter Wynton Marsalis, a superstar of jazz with impeccable credentials in the classical field. In 1984, he became the first instrumentalist in the history of the Grammy awards to win in both categories.

RIGHT:
Before he became Canada's hottest pop star, critics labelled Bryan Adams a bargain-basement Bruce Springsteen. But Adams gradually carved out a more mature image, and his foot-stomping teen anthems gave way to socially conscious ballads.

OPPOSITE:
Combining a devotional love of the late Patsy Cline with her own kinetic, cow-punk brand of country music, singer k.d. lang blew out of Consort, Alberta, to take Nashville by storm. In the process, she won fans of all musical persuasions with a unique sound that she called "torch-and-twang."

ABOVE:
In music and video, David Byrne stood out as a quirky adventurer.

ABOVE RIGHT:
Refreshingly old-fashioned, singers Sharon, Lois & Bram won the hearts of children and parents alike. With their elephant at their side, the Canadian trio became international stars in the world of kids' entertainment.

RIGHT:
Androgynous beauty Annie Lennox became an alluring icon of the 1980s, a singer whose high-powered vocals sent the hypnotic sounds of the Eurythmics soaring to the top of the charts.

A cross between Betty Boop and Marilyn Monroe, Madonna had an almost cartoonish sex appeal. But throughout the 1980s, the stylish pop starlet commanded attention for the blatant way in which she mixed images, both sacred and profane. Whether sporting a crucifix and a corset, or singing about virgins and prayers, Madonna proved to be a most provocative star.

With its lead singer, Boy George, Culture Club enjoyed phenomenal success: its debut album in 1982 was the first since The Beatles' to have three top-ten singles. But the music was overshadowed by Boy George's gender-bending fashion.

THE FACES OF DANCE

RIGHT:
Soviet-born ballet superstar Mikhail Baryshnikov, artistic director of the American Ballet Theatre and star of the movie *White Nights*, was the reigning Lord of Dance.

BELOW:
Canadian choreographer Robert Desrosiers dazzled audiences with his surreal *Blue Snake*.

OPPOSITE:
Canada's prima ballerina Karen Kain, who won international acclaim for her dramatic intensity and flawless technique, celebrated her twentieth anniversary as a member of the National Ballet with a gala performance in 1988.

STARS OF THE STAGE

In 1982, when Canada's Kate Nelligan appeared in *Plenty* on the New York stage, *The New York Times* challenged any actor to match her performance that season. Throughout the decade, Nelligan distinguished herself as one of the leading actresses of her generation.

OPPOSITE:
British composer Andrew Lloyd Webber was a multimillion-dollar music man, captivating audiences with such wildly successful creations as (*clockwise*) *The Phantom of the Opera, Cats* and *Starlight Express.*

ABOVE:
Audiences at the 1981 Toronto Theatre Festival, and later in Los Angeles, were captivated by *Tamara*, a melodrama about sex, art and fascism. The unconventional staging of this ''living movie'' had theatregoers following the action throughout a mansion.

Melding slapstick and emotion, Heath Lamberts emerged as the clown prince and comic genius of the Canadian stage in the 1980s. As Cyrano de Bergerac, he nosed his way into the limelight at the Shaw Festival.

LEFT:
The failed romance between the charismatic Pierre Elliott Trudeau and his flower-child bride, Margaret Sinclair, was pure theatre — especially in the 1980 hit *Maggie and Pierre*. At twenty-six, Linda Griffiths wrote and starred in the brilliant one-woman show about the tempestuous Trudeaus.

BELOW:
Eric Peterson starred as Canada's most famous First World War air ace in John Gray's successful musical *Billy Bishop Goes to War*.

MOVIES AND MEMORIES

Tom Berenger and Willem Dafoe starred in Oliver Stone's Oscar-winning *Platoon*, a shattering examination of the Vietnam War at close range.

Meryl Streep was the consummate actress of the decade, tackling a variety of difficult roles and accents and winning an Oscar for *Sophie's Choice* (1982), with Peter MacNicol and Kevin Kline.

Rain Man (1988) swept the Academy Awards, a tribute to the virtuoso performances of Tom Cruise as a fast-talking salesman and Dustin Hoffman as his brother, an autistic savant.

148

TOP:
The Grey Fox, starring
Jackie Burroughs and Richard
Farnsworth, was one of the first
dramatic features from English
Canada to win international
acclaim.

RIGHT:
Quebec director Denys Arcand
won eight Genie awards and an
Oscar nomination for his 1986
sex comedy *The Decline of the
American Empire* and wide
acclaim for *Jesus of Montreal*
in 1989.

BELOW:
After the $100-million success of
The Fly, Toronto director David
Cronenberg made a disturbing
drama about twin gynecologists.
Dead Ringers, starring Jeremy
Irons, appeared on most critics'
top-ten lists in 1988.

TOP:
With his respect for dramatic literacy, Canada's most prominent director, Norman Jewison, continued to excel throughout the Eighties with *A Soldier's Story*, *Agnes of God* and, especially, *Moonstruck*, a romantic comedy starring Cher and Nicolas Cage.

LEFT:
The winner of four Academy Awards in 1981, *Chariots of Fire* told the story of two men's lives and their competition in the 1924 Olympics. Produced by wunderkind David Puttnam, *Chariots of Fire* was one of the first signs of a remarkable revival in the British film industry.

BELOW:
Swedish director Lasse Hallström's 1985 movie, *My Life as a Dog*, charmed audiences with its tragicomic view of adolescence.

ABOVE:
A typically frothy comedy of the Eighties, *Splash* offered a witty fantasy about a day-dreaming New Yorker (Tom Hanks) who falls madly in love with a beautiful mermaid (Daryl Hannah).

RIGHT:
Ben Kingsley won an Oscar for his first film performance, the title role in Sir Richard Attenborough's 1982 epic biography, *Gandhi*.

OPPOSITE:
One critic described the movie *Fatal Attraction* as ''the most effective deterrent to illicit sex since stoning.'' Glenn Close starred as a knife-wielding single woman who terrorizes her married ex-lover and his family in one of the most talked-about films of the decade.

ABOVE:
Robert Redford's *Ordinary People* (1980) provided a searing depiction of a family coming apart at the seams. Donald Sutherland and Mary Tyler Moore starred as parents grieving for their dead son, while Timothy Hutton gave a riveting performance as the guilt-ridden child who survived.

RIGHT:
The Big Chill traded on baby-boom nostalgia, charting that generation's awkward — and reluctant — coming of age. A feel-good movie with a sound track of classic Motown hits, it raised the profile of such talents as Kevin Kline and Glenn Close.

BELOW RIGHT:
Debra Winger and Shirley MacLaine starred in the 1983 tearjerker *Terms of Endearment*, playing a daughter and her widowed mother struggling with issues of independence and identity.

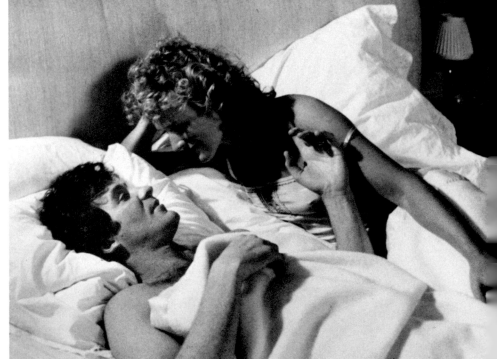

Back to the Future captivated audiences with its bizarre premise: a teenager travels back in time only to find that the young woman who falls in love with him is his future mother. The popular 1985 movie became a major vehicle for Canada's Michael J. Fox as the time-traveller desperate to ensure that history unfolds as it must, for the sake of his own survival.

BELOW:
A giddy concoction spiced with sly humor and glazed with supernatural slime, *Ghostbusters* became one of the top-grossing comedies in history. Ivan Reitman's 1984 movie, starring Bill Murray and Dan Aykroyd, went on to haunt the public with two TV cartoon adaptations, a line of toys and other spin-offs, and a movie sequel, *Ghostbusters II.*

ABOVE:
With *The Untouchables*, *No Way Out* and *Bull Durham*, Kevin Costner emerged as the leading man of the late Eighties, a matinee idol who could look smart, sound tough and smolder when necessary.

RIGHT:
Steven Spielberg's Indiana Jones was one of the most popular cinematic superheroes of all time. Beginning with *Raiders of the Lost Ark* in 1981, Harrison Ford donned his dusty fedora as the adventurer in three blockbuster hits.

OPPOSITE:
Rambo was a muscle-bound killing machine, making mincemeat of his box-office competitors. In three Rambo extravaganzas, Sylvester Stallone starred as the Vietnam vet, giving new meaning to the word *macho* and millions of bloodthirsty viewers their money's worth.

Along with such movies as *After Hours* and *Desperately Seeking Susan*, *Something Wild* signalled a new Eighties style of movie: hip, urban and irreverent. It also helped launch the career of Melanie Griffith, who went on to win rave reviews in Mike Nichols's *Working Girl*.

BELOW:
Robert DeNiro delivered a devastating, Oscar-winning performance as American boxer Jake LaMotta in Martin Scorsese's *Raging Bull*.

ABOVE LEFT:
Two of Hollywood's most gifted actresses, Jodie Foster and Kelly McGillis, starred in *The Accused* (1988), the agonizing story of a gang rape and its aftermath. Foster won an Oscar for her searing performance as the victim who fought back.

ABOVE:
Australia's *"Crocodile" Dundee*, starring the immensely popular Paul Hogan ("G'day") and Linda Kozlowski, became the most successful foreign film ever released in North America.

LEFT:
Having first made his mark on the small screen as a swaggering, salty-tongued comedian on *Saturday Night Live*, Eddie Murphy became one of Hollywood's top attractions, the foul-mouthed bad boy in such blockbuster movies as *48 Hours* and *Beverly Hills Cop*.

TEN YEARS OF TELEVISION

RIGHT:
As the nasty Alexis Carrington, Joan Collins bared her teeth and her cleavage on *Dynasty*, one of the most popular and durable prime-time soaps.

BELOW:
Mark Twain called her "the dearest and most lovable child in fiction since the immortal Alice." In 1985 Canada's most enduring literary heroine made a triumphant transition to television, with Megan Follows starring as L. M. Montgomery's irrepressible Anne of Green Gables.

OPPOSITE:
By the end of the decade, millions of middle-class baby boomers put their children to bed and escaped into *thirtysomething*, the yuppie soap opera in which Hope (Mel Harris), Michael (Ken Olin) and their friends sailed the stormy seas of mid-life.

Television began to mirror the reality of the Eighties: one of the most popular sitcoms, *Kate & Allie,* starred Susan Saint James (left) and Jane Curtin as divorced mothers raising their children under one roof.

BELOW:
An international hit, Canada's *Degrassi Junior High* won high praise for its frank portrayal of teenage life.

LEFT:
Few shows earned a more loyal following than *Hill Street Blues*. Starring Daniel J. Travanti and Veronica Hamel, it charted the drama of a ghetto-area police force.

LEFT BELOW:
It was one of the most pressing questions of 1980: Who shot J. R.? The amoral tycoon J. R. Ewing (Larry Hagman) survived and continued to plague Sue Ellen (Linda Gray), becoming one of the most durable villains of the 1980s.

ABOVE RIGHT:
Miami Vice turned struggling actor Don Johnson into a major sex symbol. The gritty police drama, co-starring Philip Michael Thomas, will be remembered as much for its influence on fashion — pastel jackets worn over T-shirts, and stubble — as for its story line.

RIGHT:
As Cliff Huxtable on *The Cosby Show* and as the best-selling author of *Fatherhood*, Bill Cosby was the father figure of the Eighties.

OPPOSITE:
In the early Eighties, more than five million fans tuned in weekly to Canada's *SCTV Network*, a brilliant parody of television, showcasing the comic genius of writer-actors Eugene Levy, Joe Flaherty, Andrea Martin and Martin Short.

Expounding the virtues of beer, bacon and "smokes," Bob (Rick Moranis) and Doug (Dave Thomas) McKenzie were the "hoser" stars of *Great White North*, giving new meaning to the term "Canadian content" and new currency to their signature "eh."

LEFT:
When two panelists began a brawl on his show in 1988, the king of tabloid TV, Geraldo Rivera, suffered a broken nose. The already controversial *Geraldo* show immediately soared in the ratings.

BELOW LEFT:
With his absurd humor and deadpan delivery, the gap-toothed host of *Late Night with David Letterman* became a cult favorite of the insomniac set.

ABOVE RIGHT:
In 1982 the CBC changed the bedtime ritual of Canadian viewers, moving *The National* with Knowlton Nash to 10 p.m. and introducing *The Journal*, the network's costliest public affairs show ever, with former radio host Barbara Frum.

RIGHT:
Donald Brittain, who died in 1989, reaffirmed his status as one of Canada's finest film-makers with his first major docudrama, *Canada's Sweetheart: The Saga of Hal C. Banks* (1985) and his six-hour epic, *The King Chronicle* (1988).

OPPOSITE:
His smoky voice and easygoing style won fans from coast to coast, helping Peter Gzowski, host of CBC Radio's *Morningside*, to become one of the best-loved broadcasters in Canada.

VISIONS OF GRANDEUR

A triumph of feminist art, *The Dinner Party* drew both adulation and scorn as it toured North America in 1982. Judy Chicago's table with thirty-nine painted plates included vaginal imagery to celebrate the role of women in myth and history.

BELOW LEFT:
American painter Eric Fischl laid bare the sexual tension in Eighties society with canvases depicting what he called ``the big subjects'' — incest, homo-sexuality, autoeroticism and the sexuality of children.

BELOW RIGHT:
In 1986 it was revealed that Andrew Wyeth had secretly painted and drawn 240 works — many of them erotic nudes — of his neighbor Helga Testorf and had sold them all for a rumored $14 million.

OPPOSITE:
The searing, razor-sharp images of Nova Scotia artist Alex Col-ville, emblems of existence for a young nation growing up, were the focus of a major retrospec-tive in 1983.

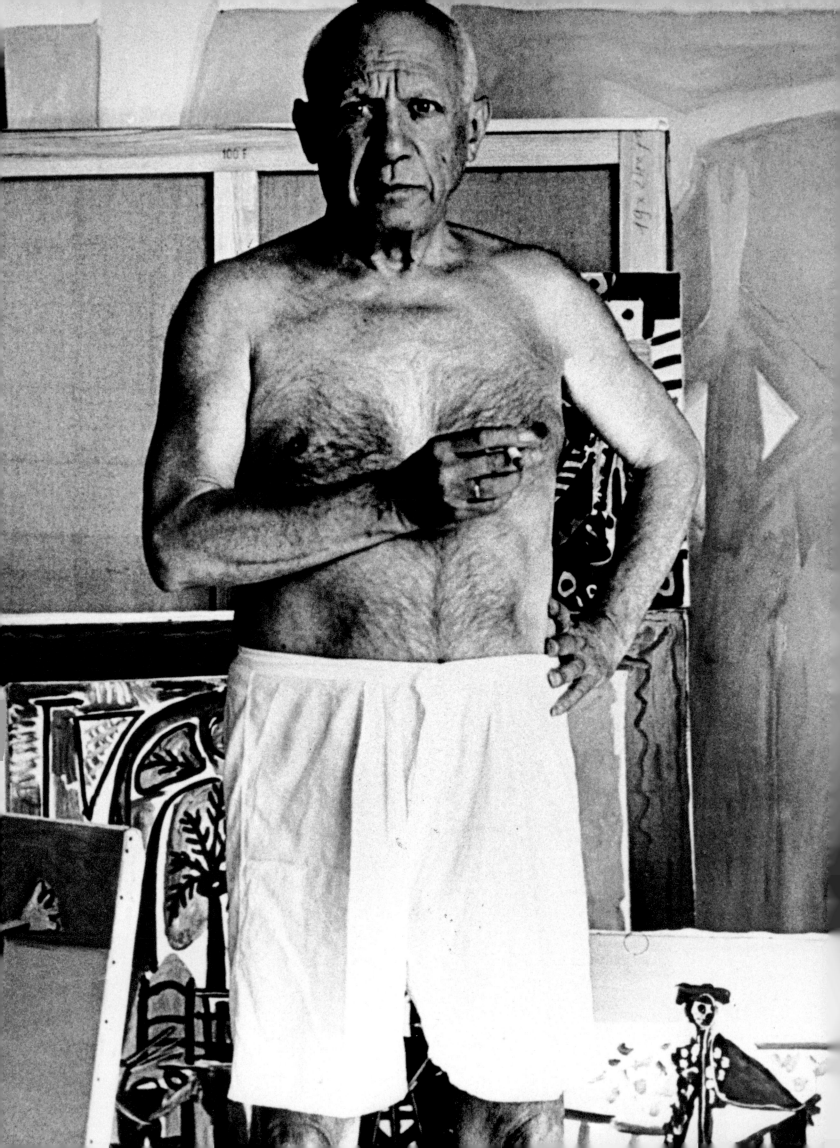

OPPOSITE:
Long after Pablo Picasso's death in 1973, the world continued to celebrate his art. In 1980 a mammoth retrospective of almost 1,000 works filled the entire exhibition space of New York City's Museum of Modern Art and broke attendance records. Another major exhibition at the Montreal Museum of Fine Arts, *Pablo Picasso: Meeting in Montreal,* was wildly popular in 1985.

TOP:
Newfoundland artists Christopher and Mary Pratt created some of the most resonant images in Canadian art, his infused with a metaphysical power, hers with a brilliant sense of the moment.

MIDDLE:
The rugged, romantic earthscapes and spatial extravaganzas of London, Ontario, painter Paterson Ewen won a dazzling reception at the Venice Biennale in 1982.

LEFT:
Canadian painter Robert Bateman achieved fame and fortune for his finely detailed portraits of nature. Some critics called him a mere illustrator, but his popularity was secure.

MASTER BUILDERS

When New York architect I. M. Pei expanded the overcrowded Louvre in Paris, he chose not to touch the venerable museum's façade, erecting instead a translucent glass pyramid. His design, completed by 1989, provoked a noisy controversy when critics attacked his modernist vision.

OPPOSITE:
Considered a prestigious symbol of urban success, Toronto's SkyDome opened in June, 1989, with great fanfare. The structure featured a 7,000-ton retractable roof — the first of its kind in the world — but it leaked. Designed by Toronto architect Roderick Robbie and structural engineer Michael Allen, the $500-million sports, concert and convention complex offered the best features of indoor and outdoor facilities.

After designing the modular housing project Habitat for Montreal's Expo 67, Moshe Safdie transformed the look of his native Israel with a number of celebrated projects, including the Holocaust Museum in Jerusalem. With his spectacularly airy National Gallery of Canada, which opened in Ottawa in 1988, Safdie put into effect once again his conviction that light provides a building with life.

FRONTIERS

Stationed in an unheated observatory on a Chilean mountaintop in 1987, Winnipeg-born astronomer Ian Shelton made history when he sighted a supernova — the light formed by the explosion of a star. It was the first such discovery near the Earth's galaxy since 1604.

BELOW:
The world welcomed the return of a celestial celebrity in 1986 as Halley's Comet came into view after completing its seventy-six-year solar orbit.

OPPOSITE:
Britain's severely disabled Stephen Hawking, considered by many the most brilliant theoretical physicist since Albert Einstein, attempted to explain the formation of the universe in his best-seller, *A Brief History of Time,* bringing science one step closer to the theory of Grand Unification.

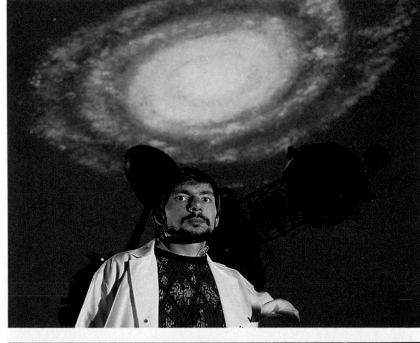

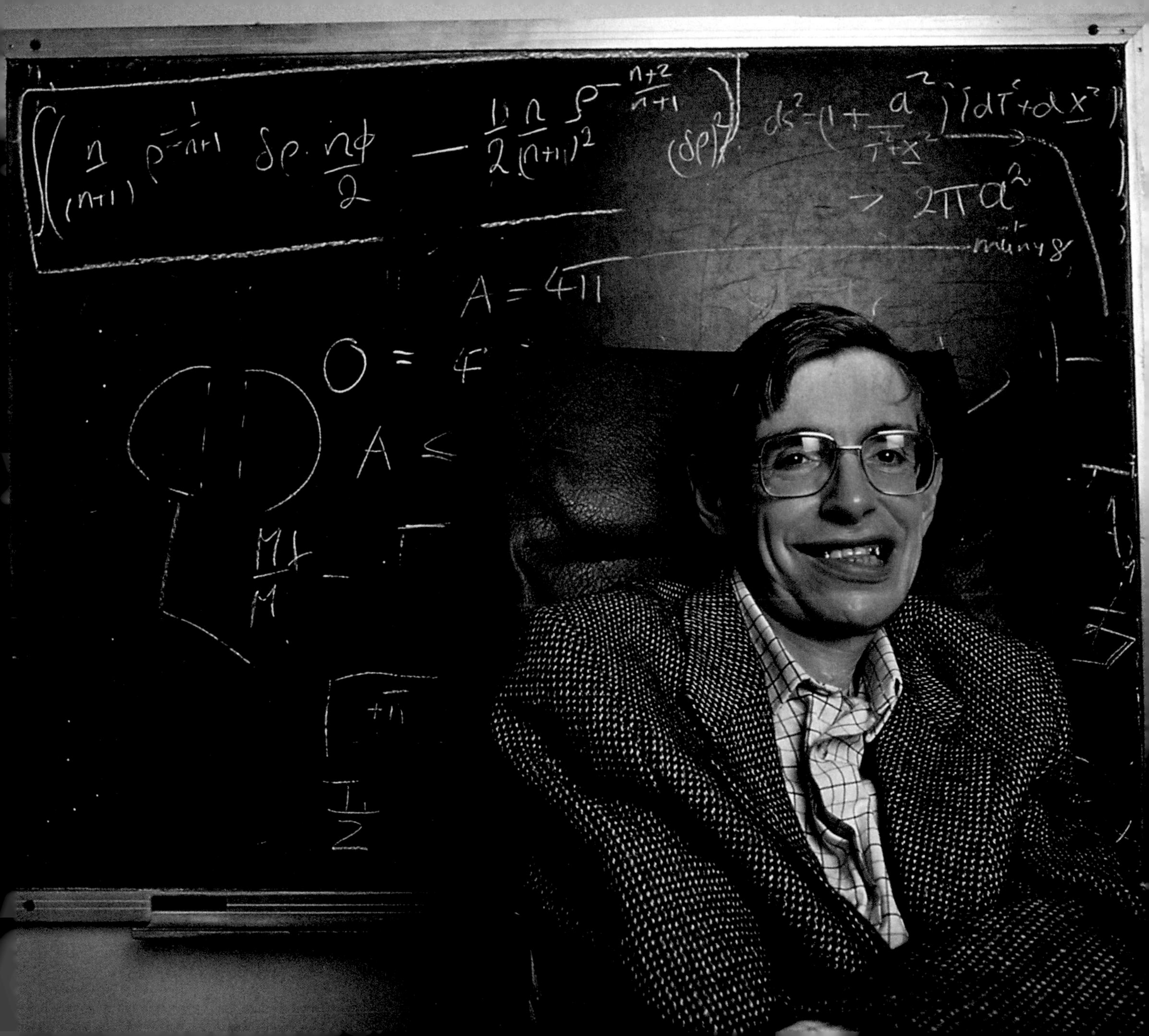

In 1986 University of Toronto chemistry professor John Polanyi won a Nobel Prize for research on molecular changes during chemical reactions. "Winning this prize is rather like being in Pompeii when Vesuvius erupted," he said. "One had a satisfaction in becoming part of history — but it did tend to interrupt the course of one's everyday life."

OPPOSITE:
On October 5, 1984, a thirty-five-year-old naval commander from Quebec City became the first Canadian astronaut in space. For eight days, Marc Garneau — the only non-American aboard the space shuttle *Challenger* — performed ten Canadian-designed experiments. His only disappointment, he said, was returning to Earth. "I could have stayed in space for two months," said Garneau. "I loved it up there."

The Canadarm, a manipulating device for U.S. space shuttles, was the highlight of Canada's space program, confirming the country's status as a leader in space technology.

Schoolteacher Christa McAuliffe was selected from more than 11,000 applicants to become the first "ordinary citizen" in space. After entering the astronaut program in preparation for the fateful *Challenger* flight in 1986, the mother of two said: "What are we doing here? We're reaching for the stars."

WHEN SCIENCE LOST ITS MAGIC

Moments before the *Challenger* explosion, Christa McAuliffe's sister and parents watched anxiously. John Glenn, the first American to orbit the Earth, later reflected, "We always knew there would be a day like this, a day we wish we could kick back forever."

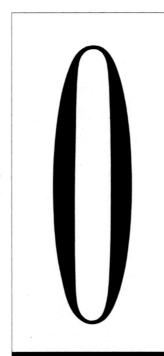

O N A COLD MORNING IN JANUARY, 1986, SEVERAL thousand people turned out in a bare Florida field to witness another routine miracle in man's conquest of the heavens. At 11:37 a.m., the space shuttle *Challenger*—astride two external booster rockets and 500,000 gallons of liquid hydrogen and oxygen—roared skyward from its launching pad. Aboard were five men and two women, one of them a thirty-seven-year-old New Hampshire schoolteacher, Christa McAuliffe. Seventy-three seconds later, *Challenger* exploded. Greed, haste and overconfidence, we later learned, had sent the shuttle aloft with imperfect joints that failed to contain the inferno inside one of its rockets. But the tragedy did not belong to America alone, any more than the sense of loss struck only the grieving families of the dead astronauts. There had been no more potent symbol of man's daring genius than the gleaming white shuttle. Before our eyes, it was reduced to smoke and raining ashes.

Rarely before had images from a mission to space so mesmerized the world. In the self-confident 1960s, there had been an air of destiny fulfilled when Neil Armstrong walked on the moon. But in the 1980s technology faltered, science lost its arrogance. Even man's greatest triumphs were strangely disquieting. In the fall of 1984, twelve-day-old Baby Fae received a transplanted animal heart. The surgical challenge was met brilliantly, but the baby died twenty days later. And the heart had been cut from a living baboon. As so often in the decade, a miracle was worked, old limits overcome and frontiers blurred. But, in the process, science raised more troubling questions than it answered. And against its biggest challenges, it failed. By the decade's end, Ronald Reagan's dream of a space-based missile defence was dead in all but name; the AIDS virus flourished unchecked.

The disillusion was not entirely justified. We demanded more than ever from technology. Surprisingly often, it delivered, and the results were sometimes dazzling. Computers acquired a human voice and learned to respond to simple speech. Artificial skin eased the unspeakable suffering of burn victims. But nothing held more breathtaking promise than the advances toward understanding the secrets of life itself. In 1980, clinical trials in London, Ontario, proved the effectiveness of a drug called cyclosporin, which inhibits the body's rejection of foreign tissue. Two years later, TV screens were filled with images of Barney Clark as he struggled, ultimately

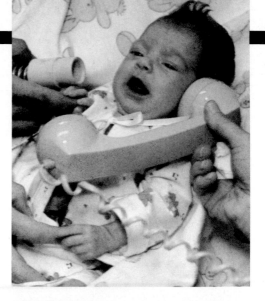

unsuccessfully, to live with a man-made heart. Another underreported event of 1980 was a decision by the U.S. Supreme Court to allow inventors of new life forms to patent their creations. Rather endearingly, the first animal to be so protected was a mouse, created at Harvard in April, 1988.

But critics saw Dr. Frankenstein disguised in the lab coats of the Harvard inventors. One opponent of genetic engineering warned that it was a short step from patented mice to patented human genes. Would we soon be able to order Bo Derek's body and Einstein's brain? Ominously, by the end of the decade a market in human parts was already under way. In August of 1988, police broke up a gang allegedly trying to smuggle Brazilian babies to North America in order to sell their organs. Six months later, British newspapers exposed a London doctor who had tried to buy kidneys from Turkish donors. Genetic engineers, in the meantime, altered the chromosomes of lowly bacteria so that they produced human insulin and growth hormone. The insulin undoubtedly saved lives. But athletes used growth hormone to cheat the clock. And, in 1987, Canadian doctors kept alive a girl without a brain so they could give her heart to a baby boy. As the decade drew to a close, what was once revered as the divine flame of human life seemed hardly more sacred than a replaceable battery. Observed Canadian historian Desmond Morton: "We have begun to feel acutely that science is not on our side. The baboon heart doesn't work. Barney Clark is dead."

The world was left to wonder what other dark possibilities were waiting to be let loose by man's impetuous curiosity. One terrifying lesson was borne on the night wind from the Ukraine in April, 1986, a wind poisoned with radiation from the ruptured nuclear reactor at Chernobyl. The meltdown occurred when technicians bungled an experiment. Then, in 1987, a New Jersey court opened a different sort of Pandora's box when it ruled that Mary Beth Whitehead had no legal claim to Baby M, the daughter she had agreed to bear for a childless couple. The gifts of knowledge, it became clear, came wrapped in new and troubling uncertainties. Whose child is the embryo conceived in a test tube? Whose life resides in an altered gene?

The rebuilt and reinforced space shuttle returned to service in 1988. But, as the decade closed, the suspicion lingered that science had gone, if not too far, then certainly into realms that demanded far greater wisdom than we had exercised in the past. It remained an open question whether fallible mankind was equal to the godlike powers of his own discovery.

— CHRIS WOOD

TOP:
After a controversial baboon-heart transplant, Baby Fae lived for only twenty days in 1984.

ABOVE:
Barney Clark made history in 1982 when he received the world's first permanent artificial heart and lived for sixteen weeks afterward.

The first Canadian expedition to Mt. Everest in 1982 began in tragedy when two icefalls killed four men. One month later, two Canadian climbers, Calgary's Laurie Skreslet and Patrick Morrow of Kimberly, B.C., reached the summit of the world's highest peak.

OPPOSITE:
In 1986 Sharon Wood of Canmore, Alberta, became the first North American woman to scale Mt. Everest. Said Wood: ''You do not know who you really are until you know what you can fully achieve.''

In 1984 University of Alberta scientists exhumed the remarkably preserved body of Petty Officer John Torrington on Beechey Island in the Canadian Arctic. The twenty-year-old member of the ill-fated Franklin expedition to find the Northwest Passage had died 138 years earlier of pneumonia. Recalled Edmonton anthropologist Owen Beattie: "After two years of planning and getting to know John Torrington and then coming face-to-face with him, it was really quite remarkable."

ABOVE:
In 1985 U.S. scientist Robert Ballard uncovered a vivid world 2½ miles beneath the surface of the Atlantic Ocean as his team captured the first images of the sunken *Titanic*'s watery grave. Recalled Ballard: "It was like landing on the moon."

A 1988 discovery of fossilized dinosaur eggs in the Gobi Desert fuelled interest in dinosaurs as scientists heatedly debated new theories about the creatures.

BUSINESS

He began as a used-car salesman in 1951, bought a dealership of his own in 1961 and slowly acquired more companies. Jimmy Pattison, the director of a merchandising and manufacturing empire, built a personal fortune worth more than $800 million — but made his real mark as the one-dollar-a-year chairman of Vancouver's highly successful Expo 86, which drew twenty-two million people from around the world.

OPPOSITE:
Donald Trump personified life in the fast track. Brash and flamboyant, his genius for real estate transactions helped him build one of the largest business empires in the United States. In 1988 alone, Trump bought the famous Plaza Hotel in New York City for $486 million and sold the St. Moritz Hotel for $185 million more than he had paid in 1985. Said Trump: ''I like playing real-life Monopoly.''

In 1985 two Alberta banks, the Canadian Commercial Bank and Northland Bank, collapsed into bankruptcy, ending Western Canada's dream of building a strong, independent financial base. After Ottawa closed the banks, opposition members called for the resignation of Barbara McDougall, then minister of state for finance, but the minister stood by the decision, saying, ''I can tell you that I still sleep at night.''

Toronto's publicity-shy Reichmann brothers emerged as one of Canada's wealthiest and most powerful families. After arriving from Europe in the 1950s, Paul and his brothers Albert and Ralph built a vast and diversified $7.6-billion empire, with energy holdings that included Canada's frontier oil and natural gas reserves and spectacular property developments such as the $7-billion Canary Wharf in London, England.

An insider trading scandal shook Japan in 1988 when an inquiry revealed that 159 politicians, bureaucrats and businessmen had made enormous profits from Recruit, a $3.9-billion information-and-real-estate company. The discovery forced the resignation of more than twenty government officials and business leaders, including Prime Minister Noboru Takeshita (*left*) in 1989.

In Hong Kong they called him ''Mr. Money'' — a sound description of Chinese billionaire Li Ka-shing, a man whose name became synonymous with the flood of Hong Kong money and immigrants into Canada. After buying Husky Oil for $473 million in 1987, Li added Vancouver's former Expo 86 site to his burgeoning empire.

THE BUSINESS OF CHANGE

Ivan Boesky was known on Wall Street as "Ivan the terrible." In 1986 investigators discovered that much of the powerful arbitrager's $370-million fortune had been accumulated through illegal insider trading. Boesky's testimony was responsible for the 1989 indictment of junk bond king Michael Milken, the central figure in the largest securities probe in U.S. history.

OR THOSE WHO SUBSCRIBE TO THE CAPITALIST ETHIC, the 1980s were less a time of change than a decade of revolution. The earth moved. This was true in London, with its "Big Bang" on October 27, 1986. The trading floor disappeared to make way for computerized buying and selling of shares, set brokerage commissions ended, and markets were suddenly open to global competition. It was also true on Wall Street, which suffered its largest one-day stock market decline on Black Monday — October 19, 1987 — as well as an ongoing credibility crisis as several star traders were led away in handcuffs. And it was true in Canada, where business replaced hockey as the country's leading spectator sport. Everything changed.

It's hard to recall now that Torontonians once fretted that Calgary might become Canada's new business centre. It's even harder to remember the once-tidy world of Bay Street, its well-ordered clans of money managers perpetuating their institutions and themselves by pedigree, instinct and fellowship. The right connections, schooling and club allegiance assured ambitious juniors a pew in the major investment houses.

Three things changed all that: globalization of the capital markets, deregulation (which allowed anyone to own anything) and, above all, the preparation for and final realization of the Free Trade Agreement with the United States. Those smug preppies in three-piece suits with mid-Atlantic accents are long gone from the scene: they're now either junior chiefs of staff in the Mulroney government or hawking BMWs to successful dentists. With the exception of Burns Fry and Richardson Greenshields, the major investment houses have also vanished as recognizable entities, becoming vaguely troublesome subsidiaries of the chartered banks.

Deregulation, which triggered these and other changes, appears to have been either a remarkably brave or a singularly stupid initiative, depending on the vantage point. In fact, we stumbled into it, and no one knew what the ultimate consequences might be. Yet it was inevitable: there was no other way to cope with the burgeoning capital pools of Japan and other world powers. Their financial institutions had already been deregulated, and others needed the extra clout of diversification to compete.

One immediate result of the new rules has been a drastic centralization of the fiscal, legal, accounting and money-making service sectors in every financial centre. That's why Toronto became the country's financial heart. By the end of the decade, three-quarters of the Canadian Establishment's certified members lived within the Toronto watershed. For better and worse, Toronto became the only Canadian city where belonging to the local elite qualified one for cross-country status. With its 100 million square feet of office space, the Ontario capital became more than twice as dominant in relation to its economic hinterland as was New York City, the home address of only 15 per cent of the Fortune 500.

The most fascinating trend was the globalization of money markets, permanently transforming the nature of Canadian business. The financial world shrank, and international borders became meaningless. Trade surpluses from Japan and other export giants turned up as commodity investments, bond holdings or money-market flips that benefited numbered bank accounts in obscure locales.

At the same time, more Canadian entrepreneurs, especially in the real estate field, ruffled the American eagle's feathers. They were so successful in purchasing premium properties that the Yanks started to worry about Snowbirds roosting in some of their most profitable nests. Toronto's Reichmann brothers transformed downtown New York, opening the $1.5-billion World Financial Centre in Battery Park in 1988 as well as modernizing half a dozen other American cities. Robert Campeau seemed determined to run up as big a debt as Brazil: his purchases included the $8.2-billion Federated Department Stores of Cincinnati, owners of Bloomingdale's. The McCain brothers from Florenceville, New Brunswick, conquered the world's french-fries market. Meanwhile, Vancouver's Jimmy Pattison, chairman of Expo 86, force-fed his private conglomerate's growth, bought a Swiss bank and hired Ronald Reagan to speak at his annual meeting.

The Darwin award for survival above and beyond the call of the bottom line was richly earned by Varity's Victor Rice. This man laid off 52,000 employees, changed his company's name from Massey-Ferguson and turned the firm inside out so that no one knew what, if anything, Varity did — all the while collecting his annual $1-million salary. Meanwhile, Conrad Black finally found his true métier buying, running and rehabilitating newspapers. He probably got the bargain of the century when he acquired London's mighty *Daily* and *Sunday Telegraph* in 1985. Peter Cole of Central Capital Corp. was the decade's itchiest acquisitor, and Mickey Cohen, now chairman of Molson's, emerged as a major corporate contender. Ted Medland, the once all-powerful chairman of Wood Gundy, put the country's most respected investment house through the humiliation of three unsuccessful mergers. He finally put himself out of his self-created misery by prematurely retiring in 1988. Jack Gallagher, whose magic in promoting the fortunes of Dome Petroleum was such that a flash of his molars was enough to raise the price of his stock, finally stopped smiling. Canada's mightiest oil explorer and most imaginative tax shelter went bust in the early 1980s.

The decade will be most dramatically remembered for Black Monday, when meltdown madness took over the stock markets, with the TSE's composite index plummeting 507 points. The Bank of Canada responded by flooding the banking system with extra liquidity, and a recession was temporarily averted. Much more significant in the long run will be the Free Trade Agreement, painfully negotiated between Canada and the United States. The profound consequences of that deal on the direction of Canadian business will become clear only as we approach the millennium and begin to develop our common-law relationship in the bed of an elephant.

—PETER C. NEWMAN

On October 19, 1987 — known as "Black Monday" — history's biggest stock market crash stunned shareholders. From Hong Kong to London, financial markets were shaken to the core, and many investors, who lost hundreds of millions of dollars, were reluctant to return to the market. Despite fears that a massive economic slump would follow, the economies of most industrialized countries remained strong.

ABOVE LEFT:
Lee Iacocca was renowned as North America's first celebrity executive, saving Chrysler Corp. from bankruptcy, and penning two best-selling books.

BELOW LEFT:
Meat-packing and sports-franchise king Peter Pocklington, who ran for the leadership of the Progressive Conservative party in 1983, was best known for a deal that most Canadians viewed as a betrayal: the trade of Edmonton Oiler Wayne Gretzky to the Los Angeles Kings.

ABOVE RIGHT:
As he propelled Peter and Edward Bronfman's Brascan to a frontline position in financial services and natural resources, Trevor Eyton refined the art of the investment banker — buying into troubled firms and turning them into winners.

RIGHT:
Max Ward established his one-aircraft Wardair in 1952 and by 1987 had transformed it into the third-largest airline in Canada. When the firm faced bankruptcy in 1989, PWA took it over.

''Smilin' Jack'' Gallagher's resignation as chairman of Dome Petroleum in 1983 marked the end of a thirty-year career at the company's helm. A visionary who led the assault on Canada's untapped Arctic oil reserves, Gallagher built Dome into one of the world's largest oil firms. In the end, the recession and falling oil prices shattered his dream — leaving Dome almost bankrupt and paving the way for its sale to Amoco Canada Petroleum.

Garth Drabinsky built North America's second-largest silver-screen empire in less than ten years, with 1,800 elegantly appointed movie theatres from Toronto to Los Angeles. Along the way, Cineplex Odeon's brash and controversial chairman fought a pitched battle, not only with competitors but with his own partners over aggressive expansion plans.

195

FAR LEFT:
Robert Campeau, owner of one of Canada's top real estate firms, began buying department store chains, and ended up becoming a dominant figure in U.S. retailing. His most notorious acquisition — the $10.9-billion purchase of Federated Department Stores Inc. of Cincinnati — set a new record as the largest takeover by a Canadian in the United States.

LEFT:
The lowly potato is not a glamorous commodity, but New Brunswick's Harrison McCain parlayed a single french-fry plant into a multinational giant, with sales exceeding $1 billion.

Millionaire oilman Frank King had the vision to bring the 1988 Winter Olympics to Calgary. Doomsayers predicted disaster, but money flowed in from sponsors, and the Games earned a profit of $46 million.

ABOVE LEFT:
Canada's press magnates
Gordon Fisher (Southam) and
Kenneth Thomson had their
knuckles rapped in 1981 when
the Kent commission recommended limiting the size of their
sprawling newspaper chains.

ABOVE RIGHT:
Australian-born billionaire
Rupert Murdoch emerged as the
newest media baron.
Determined to own the world's
largest communications empire,
he purchased *The Times* of
London, *The Sun*, *TV Guide* and
*The Hong Kong South China
Morning Post*, among others.

Loquacious tycoon Conrad Black
dealt away his oil companies
and grocery stores in the early
1980s and built an international
media empire that included
Saturday Night magazine and
London's *Daily Telegraph*.

ABOVE LEFT:
Montreal journalists Scott Abbott and Chris Haney created Trivial Pursuit while playing Scrabble, and their game became a household word in the Eighties, taxing the memories of millions around the world. The game, which was available in eight different editions in twenty-seven countries, made them exceedingly rich and famous.

BELOW LEFT:
Steve Jobs was the whiz-kid of the computer boom after designing the Apple computer at twenty-three. But his vision of building a corporate countercul-ture in California's Silicon Valley ended in 1985 when Apple's management, responding to declining sales and poor morale, relieved him of his responsibilities. Like all personal computer manufacturers, Apple was hard pressed to fight IBM's dominance of the market.

He was the king of franchising
and a hamburger diplomat.
After building a chain of 560
McDonald's restaurants across
Canada, George Cohon,
the ebullient president of
McDonald's Canada, began his
march on Eastern Europe,
opening outlets in Belgrade and
Budapest. His proudest moment
took place in 1988, when he
signed a deal with Moscow's
city council to erect twenty
pairs of golden arches in the
Soviet capital, the first one on
Gorky Street near Red Square.

OPPOSITE:
They were known as the
"amazing Ghermezians." In
the early Eighties, the four
brothers redefined indoor
shopping when they built the
cavernous West Edmonton Mall
— with its simulated beach, a
twenty-five-ride amusement
park, golf course and more than
800 stores under one roof.

THE HUNGRY AND THE HOMELESS

By 1984 laborer Claude Beaudry had been out of work for more than a year and no longer qualified for unemployment insurance. His Sudbury, Ontario, family, like many other Canadians, suffered financially and psychologically in the wake of the recession.

BELOW:
The devastating recession in the early 1980s was Canada's worst since the Depression of the 1930s. Thousands of workers across the country lost their jobs, hundreds of families lost their homes and many drifted across the nation in search of work. Lineups at food banks were a vivid symbol of the depth of the economic slowdown.

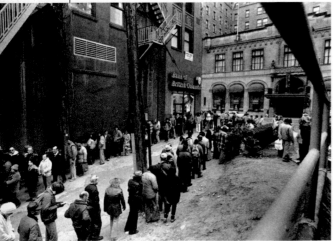

Bob White, the dynamic leader of the Canadian Auto Workers, won international recognition for his refusal to accept U.S. direction on the Chrysler strike in 1982. Then, three years later, he broke away from one of North America's most powerful unions, the 1.2-million-member United Auto Workers, and fundamentally altered unionism in Canada.

PREVIOUS PAGES:
Government reports called it "rural depopulation," but for Canada's agricultural community, the 1980s were a painful time of despair. Hit by record interest rates, falling crop prices and drought, many farmers were forced into bankruptcy.

On June 1, 1986, 1,080 workers at the Gainers meat-packing plant in Edmonton walked off the job, beginning one of the most violent strikes in recent Canadian history.

BELOW:
In 1988, Britain experienced a huge upsurge in militant union activity. More than 6,000 nurses and other health care workers used week-long work stoppages to protest low wages.

THE SPORTING LIFE

ABOVE:
The "Drive of '85" became the "Dive of '85" when the Toronto Blue Jays, widely rated as baseball's most talented team in the mid-1980s, lost the last three games of a best-of-seven American League pennant series to the Kansas City Royals. The Royals went on to beat the St. Louis Cardinals four games to three and win the World Series.

The pre-eminent hockey player of the decade, Wayne Gretzky led the Edmonton Oilers to four Stanley Cup victories and Team Canada to beat the Soviet Union in the 1987 Canada Cup tournament — an achievement he called "my greatest thrill."

It was a dream come true for Ottawa figure skater Elizabeth Manley, who stole the show at the 1988 Winter Games in Calgary, skating her way to a silver medal. "It sounded like the world caving in," crowed Manley. "I could have stayed out there all night."

LEFT:
Toronto Blue Jays left-fielder George Bell, the volatile all-star hitter voted the American League's most valuable player in 1987, tailed off in 1988 after he angrily refused to give up his left field and confine his role largely to serving as the team's designated hitter.

BOTTOM LEFT:
San Francisco 49ers' Joe Montana proved to be one of the best quarterbacks in football history, leading his team to three Superbowl wins in the decade.

TOP RIGHT:
The Montreal Expos, a dead-end team for most of the decade, came to life in 1989, led by the inspired pitching of Mark Langston.

RIGHT:
Pittsburgh Penguins centre Mario Lemieux demonstrated his star quality during the 1987 Canada Cup series — and became the likely challenger to Wayne Gretzky's supremacy.

In 1985 Michael Spinks made boxing history, becoming the first light-heavyweight champion ever to win the heavyweight title, dethroning seven-year champion Larry Holmes.

OPPOSITE:
They were known as the Crazy Canucks, a group of daredevils who created a sensation on the World Cup ski circuit during the early 1980s. The stars were Ken Read (*right*), who placed second on the 1980 World Cup circuit, and Steve Podborski, who made history in 1982 by becoming the first North American to win the prestigious World Cup title.

A fierce competitor, Mike Tyson became the youngest heavyweight boxing champion in history when, at the age of twenty, he defeated Trevor Berbick in Las Vegas for the World Boxing Council title.

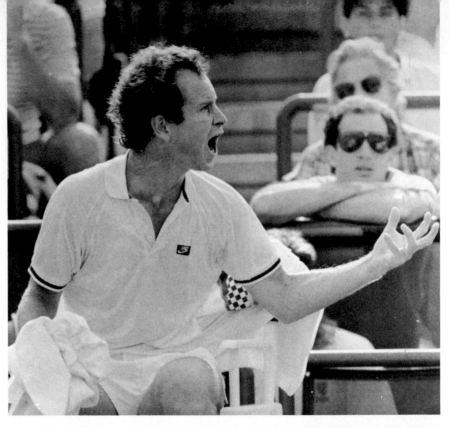

He pouted, spat, yelled and broke his racket. John McEnroe (*above*) was the bad boy of tennis, a petulant, temperamental challenger to Bjorn Borg's domination of men's singles tennis. The Swede beat the American at Wimbledon in 1980 — winning his fifth consecutive title — but when McEnroe won in 1981, Borg never returned. McEnroe took two of the next three championships and gained added attention when he married actress Tatum O'Neal. Borg, on the other hand, was divorced twice and in early 1989 was hospitalized for an overdose of barbiturates.

In 1983 Canada's ''Darling'' Carling Bassett pushed Chris Evert to the brink of defeat in the Florida Virginia Slims Tournament.

For nine years American tennis star Chris Evert (*above*) dominated the women's world singles circuit. But in 1982 her longtime opponent, Czechoslovak-born Martina Navratilova (*above left*), claimed the number one spot, reigning until 1987, when she lost to West Germany's Steffi Graf.

DENNIS CONNER
JUDY CONNER

OPPOSITE:
In 1988 U.S. yachtsman Dennis Conner won his fourth America's Cup aboard a sleek blue catamaran — the first of its kind in the history of the race. But the following year, his victory on *Stars & Stripes* was discounted by a judge, who ruled that the boat — which weighed only 6,000 pounds compared to his competitor's 83,000-pound yacht — violated the spirit of the competition.

ABOVE:
Spain's Seve Ballesteros was the decade's most gifted and most appealing golfer, winning the Masters in 1980 and 1983 and the British Open in 1984 and 1988.

LEFT:
As wrestling captivated the public in the mid-1980s, Hulk Hogan, pictured with television's Mr. T., became a hero of the masses.

216

Argentina's Diego Maradona, arguably the best soccer player of the decade, led his national team to victory in the 1986 World Cup Tournament.

BELOW:
It was a grisly incident that shocked the world. At the 1985 European Cup soccer match in Brussels, heavy-drinking British fans attacked rival Italians with bottles and iron bars. The death toll: thirty-eight, with more than 300 injured.

Earvin Johnson, more aptly known as Magic, was finally honored in 1987. After eight outstanding seasons, the Los Angeles Lakers guard was named the National Basketball Association's most valuable player.

The Boston Celtics' Larry Bird, a basketball superstar since 1979, was Magic Johnson's prime rival for most of the decade.

Canada's Gilles Villeneuve was a Grand Prix favorite, an aggressive perfectionist who came first six times on the circuit. But during qualifying runs for the 1982 Belgian Grand Prix, he died when his Ferrari collided with another car.

GUTS, GOLD AND GLORY

Eleven months after he broke his ankle during a training session, Canadian skater Gaetan Boucher sped to glory at the 1984 Winter Olympics in Sarajevo, taking home two gold medals and a bronze.

OPPOSITE:

Canadian swimmer Alex Baumann broke his own world records, winning two gold medals and a silver at the 1984 Los Angeles Olympics. At the Games, boycotted by the Soviet Union, East Germany and thirteen other nations, Canada won an unprecedented forty-three medals, ten of them gold.

It was the most memorable image of the Los Angeles Olympics in 1984. American track star Mary Decker, leading in the 3,000-metre race, fell after barefoot Zola Budd, running for Britain, edged past her. Decker, enraged, accused Budd of cutting her off.

OPPOSITE:
It was billed as "the battle of the Brians," the culmination of a ten-year rivalry between two world champions. In the end, despite the cheering of a wildly partisan crowd at the 1988 Calgary Olympics, American Brian Boitano (*middle*) won the gold medal in men's figure skating, and Canada's Brian Orser (*left*) went home with the silver.

ABOVE:
Italian skier Alberto (La Bomba) Tomba, who won two gold medals in Calgary, described himself as "the new messiah of skiing."

In her final faceoff with American Debi Thomas, East Germany's Katarina Witt won the gold medal in 1988.

OPPOSITE:
Laurie Graham was Canada's most successful female skier of the decade, renowned as a fearless downhill racer and winner of six World Cup races. But her fifth-place finish at the Calgary Olympics was a disappointing finale to a remarkable career.

With her two bronze medals, Canada's Karen Percy was the only non-European medallist in the alpine ski events. In the downhill race, she had the added distinction of beating Swiss superstars Maria Walliser and Michela Figini.

BELOW:
Britain's Eddie "The Eagle" Edwards placed last in ski jumping and first in crowd-pleasing at the Calgary Olympics.

One of the most theatrical events at the Calgary Olympics was the ice-dance competition. Soviet veterans Natalia Bestemianova and Andrei Bukin (*left below*), silver medallists at Sarajevo in 1984, won the gold medal for their tempestuous, passionate performance. Canada's Tracy Wilson and Robert McCall (*opposite*) charmed the crowd with their lightning footwork, winning the bronze. But it was the Quebec brother-and-sister team of Isabelle and Paul Duchesnay (*left above*), representing France, who stole the show, shocking the judges and wooing the crowd with a seductive, unorthodox routine.

The superstars of the World Cup circuit, Swiss skiers Pirmin Zurbriggen and Peter Müller, won only three medals at the Calgary Olympics.

OPPOSITE:
Alberta's Kurt Browning skated out of Brian Orser's shadow in 1989 when he won the men's world championship. Browning dazzled a crowd of 7,000 with his trademark quadruple toe loop and stunning jumps. Browning's victory provided badly needed encouragement to Canadian athletes after sprinter Ben Johnson's disgrace at the Seoul Olympics six months earlier. Said Browning: "Maybe this will give Canadians the opportunity to cheer again."

SILENCE IN THE STANDS

According to Ben Johnson, coach Charlie Francis advised the sprinter to take steroids.

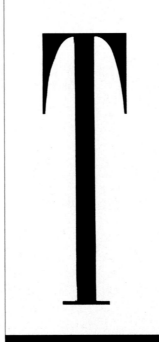

THEY WERE SUPERMEN, MEETING IN THE CONTEST OF the decade, some said the century. The arena was the heroic oval of Seoul's Olympic Stadium. The event was the most elemental in sport — the 100-metre dash. Eight runners lined up at the starting blocks on that sunny afternoon in September, 1988. But the eyes of the world were on only two: Canadian Ben Johnson, stocky and inarticulate, and American Carl Lewis, as slim and polished as any star in Hollywood. Then the starter's pistol barked, and in 9.79 seconds Johnson left Lewis in the distance and redefined the limit of human speed.

Three days later, the wonder and elation dissolved in the bitter realization that Johnson's dazzling victory owed as much to chemistry as to training. A test revealed traces of a banned synthetic sex hormone in the runner's urine. The revelation cost Johnson his Olympic gold medal and his reputation. It cost much of the sports world its innocence. Months afterward, a judicial inquiry documented the disheartening evidence that Ben Johnson epitomized the flawed ethics of a decade when it seemed winning was everything.

It really should not have come as such a surprise. The events in Seoul had been foreshadowed by open speculation in the late 1970s that Eastern Bloc athletes routinely used drugs to improve their performances. If they did, they were seldom caught. But then, at the Pan American Games in Caracas in 1983, laboratory tests proved beyond question that nineteen athletes, including two Canadians, had reinforced their talent with chemicals. At the 1984 Summer Olympics in Los Angeles eleven more athletes were exposed. That same year, after winning a silver medal at the Winter Games in Sarajevo, Yugoslavia, Finnish cross-country skier Aki Karvonen confessed that he had improved his endurance by removing a quantity of his own blood weeks before the competition and reinfusing it at the last minute — an undetectable technique known as blood-doping.

By then, according to Johnson's coach, Charlie Francis, the sprinter had been using steroids for three years and he would continue for most of the decade. In the United States, the same synthetic hormones were being passed around the locker rooms of college and professional football teams. In 1987 West German heptathlete Birgit Dressel died unexpectedly of an acute allergic reaction to the more than one dozen drugs in her system. "These are harmless," she

had reassured her mother not long before her death. "All athletes take them." If not all, then certainly far more than the sports world ever acknowledged. Indeed, according to International Olympic Committee vice-president Richard Pound, "there could either have been positive tests that were not acted upon by the International Amateur Athletic Federation or a direction not to test for certain substances." And competitors were not the only users. By 1988 steroids had become as popular as linament in neighborhood gyms where policemen, body builders and models of both sexes pursued the perfect physique.

But it was, after all, the Eighties, the decade when image became substance and greed was glorified. Even the Kremlin conceded, in the spirit of *perestroika*, that wealth was virtuous. And the pressure on athletes to win at any price was overwhelming. Those who reached the Olympics carried with them the knowledge that they were surrogate warriors in the rivalry of nations and that only medals counted in the tallies kept by press and public. It was winners, not good sportsmen, who attracted the lavish courtship of commercial sponsors. In a decade that seemed to value little else, the scent of fame and fortune held a powerful allure. As a young man of scant education and few skills, Ben Johnson was barely employable; as the fastest man in the world, he was worth $10 million in commercial-endorsement contracts.

A 1987 world record in the 100-metre dash earned Ben Johnson a fortune in endorsements.

By 1988 the accumulation of scandals led Canada to join the United States, the Soviet Union and more than a hundred other nations in drafting a plan to test international competitors more frequently for drug use. But by then athletes had found new catalysts of strength and speed that were even harder to detect than the old ones. Human growth hormone produced in laboratories could not be distinguished from the body's own. Other compounds hid the telltale urine trace of cruder drugs. As for the avarice that fed the age, its motive force was undiminished.

In the end, the decade closed with the most troubling issues unresolved. Where, after all, was the line between fair and foul in the pursuit of the ideals of the Olympic motto: *Citius, Altius, Fortius*—Faster, Higher, Stronger? And even if the moral line was drawn, it still left the significance of the records set in the 1980s in doubt. Johnson often insisted that his speed was entirely his own; the residue of doubt left by his downfall tarnished the accomplishments of many other athletes. It was that, finally, that struck most deeply at the tenuous bond uniting crowd and competitor. Johnson had cheated not only the seven men beside him on the track but the millions who cheered him to the finish line. After Seoul, they would never watch a race the same way again.

—CHRIS WOOD

With her outrageous costumes — referred to as "athletic lingerie" — the flamboyant U.S. sprinter Florence (Flo-Jo) Griffith-Joyner was a show-stopper at the Seoul Olympics, winning three gold medals.

Three times a world champion in synchronized swimming, Cana-da's Carolyn Waldo won two Olympic golds in the balletic event at Seoul in 1988: solo, and duet with Michelle Cameron.

SIGNS OF THE TIMES

Day care became a huge concern as the number of two-income families increased dramatically.

BELOW:
In the Age of Greed, the aptly named Robin Leach celebrated the conspicuous consumption of famous personalities on his syndicated television show, *Lifestyles of the Rich and Famous.*

OPPOSITE:
Whether in search of past lives or a quicker route to happiness, thousands joined the New Age movement. One of the major gurus, actress Shirley MacLaine, talked about the healing powers of crystals, the body's energy points, astral guides and past-life regression.

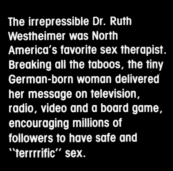

The irrepressible Dr. Ruth
Westheimer was North
America's favorite sex therapist.
Breaking all the taboos, the tiny
German-born woman delivered
her message on television,
radio, video and a board game,
encouraging millions of
followers to have safe and
``terrrrific'' sex.

ABOVE:
She was the high priestess of health, pricking the conscience of an overweight and sluggish society. In two best-selling books, *New York Times* columnist Jane Brody preached the gospel of carbohydrates and total fitness. Her followers were devout, and Brody became a millionaire in the process.

At times, it seemed that taste was all that mattered — the taste of blueberry vinegar, kiwi mousse and green peppercorns. Food became a luxury item, and no self-respecting yuppie went without the *Silver Palate* cookbooks, the best-selling bibles of food preparation by New Yorkers Julee Rosso and Sheila Lukins.

THE GADGETS OF AN ERA

The cellular telephone, the microwave oven and the video cassette player became vital symbols of success in the Eighties.

I N THE 1980 FEDERAL ELECTION CAMPAIGN, MANY TRAV-elling journalists exchanged their trusted portable type-writers for suitcase-sized computer terminals. The new machines, designed to transmit reports by telephone, were supposed to be more efficient than the old meth-ods of telegraph or dictation. Those first portable ter-minals were bulky, often balky and needed electrical power. They also required the user to adjust to new keyboards, learn computer-code languages — and be more patient than during the pre-electronic news pro-cess that began, according to legend, with the report-er's call: "Hiya, sweetheart, get me rewrite."

Four years later, the computer revolution finally pushed the typewriter reporter, the rewrite desk and mechanical typesetting into history. For the 1984 elec-tion, journalism's new tools were battery-powered lap-top terminals. With a built-in transmitter and telephone couplers, a story could now be sent in seconds from the nearest pay phone into the home-office computer—and almost as quickly into print anywhere in the world. By the 1988 election, the cellular telephone and portable facsimile transmitter hit the campaign trail. In the same eight-year span of the 1980s, television production advanced from cumbersome film cameras to compact videocams, which could send sound and pictures, via a mobile satellite dish, almost directly into a nightly newscast.

The easier, speedier way of disseminating news was only part of a communications explosion during a decade that also transformed work methods, education, recreation and everyday living. Earning, learning or just living increasingly became a matter of circulating information in words and pictures, numbers or music. In an atmosphere of relentless change, employers, teachers and parents, as well as politicians and journalists, were pressed to adjust to a world in which the human attention span seemed to shrink under the information flood.

Marshall McLuhan, who once predicted that electronic communications would transform the world into a global village, offered an observation on the bombardment of the senses. He said, "In the instantaneous age of information, or the age of instantaneous information, a point of view is meaningless." According to McLuhan, the electronic media of communication are so potent and disturbing because they are, in effect, extensions of the human nervous system, and totally involve the mind and senses with the outside world.

If so, the 1980s offered many new ways to get involved. As both communication tools and

RIGHT:
RIGHT:
The VCR revolutionized leisure habits in the Eighties: with the push of a button, viewers could program an aerobics class, a Hollywood feature or last week's sitcom. And before learning to read, a new generation learned how to press "play."

BELOW:
Personal computers transformed every aspect of life — from professional and political to educational and recreational — as the world became computer literate.

playthings, the names of the new gadgets became household words: PCs (personal computers), VCRs (video cassette recorders), CDs (compact-disc players), auto-focus cameras, camcorders, cellular phones and the fax (facsimile). Soft-touch calculators barely thicker than a credit card performed almost as much arithmetic as the earliest electronic digital computer — a clanking 1946 monster the size of a two-car garage. Automobile dashboards began to utter advice in electronic simulations of a human voice. On freight trains, computers replaced the crews in the caboose. Sound raced with the speed of light — translated into laser pulses — on new fibre-optic telephone channels. By punching a series of numbers on a bank's wall computer, a customer received instant cash. In New York City, singles even flirted by fax, using a dating service that menaced the slower, more circumspect matchmaking methods of the classified ad or the singles club.

Statistics Canada recorded that, in the middle of 1988, more than half of Canadian households had VCRs, almost 13 per cent had PCs, 8 per cent CDs and 3 per cent camcorders — all items that were either unavailable or too rare to rate mention in its reports on household facilities at the outset of the decade. Next, and already in prototype form: telephone attachments that tell in advance where a call is coming from, terminals that immerse the operator in a three-dimensional world of sensations, so-called hot-electron transistors with five times the speed of present models, and laser-circuit supercomputers that pack the power of present mainframes the size of a filing cabinet into an instrument no bigger than a telephone answering machine. McLuhan, who died on the last day of 1980 and whose ideas received renewed attention in a spate of publications toward the end of the decade, said, "My work predicts what has already happened." But what happened in the 1980s reinforced his prophesies on the impact of the information explosion, and shrank the global village to a sensitive, high-speed hamlet.

—CARL MOLLINS

She told her fans to "feel the burn," and burn they did: millions around the world put on tights and bounced around their living rooms to Jane Fonda's exercise videos. When reports warned that high-impact aerobics could cause injuries, the actress quickly responded, cheerleading her fans through a low-impact workout. Above all, Fonda offered living proof that exercise could make a difference.

OPPOSITE:
Manufacturers transformed the lowly running shoe into a state-of-the-art commodity as millions joined the jogging craze, rising early for a solitary run with their Walkmans or falling in step with the throng at a marathon race.

IN THEIR OWN FASHION

Their label was one of the most sought-after in a label-obsessed decade. Don Green and Michael Budman dominated the popular market with Roots, a line of casual- and leather-wear that became the uniform of preppies, yuppies and, by the middle of the decade, the babies of the affluent.

BELOW:
The miniskirt made a comeback in the Eighties, reappearing often in black leather — a staple of many wardrobes.

OPPOSITE:
Black leather coupled with rainbow-colored hair or a shaved head were the trademarks of 1980s punk style.

As the decade progressed, professional women adopted a more assertive look, with shoulder pads, blazers and trench coats as part of the uniform.

Toronto fashion designer Alfred Sung became world-renowned for his classic, sophisticated styles.

THE CHANGING FAMILY LIFE

The newest consumer item for working parents — and one of the hardest to come by — was day care.

T IS DINNER HOUR IN THE LATE EIGHTIES. AS THE FILI-pino nanny finishes her day, Dad pops a Lean Cuisine Lasagna Verde into the microwave. Sitting in front of the television, watching a taped episode of *Teenage Mutant Ninja Turtles*, Junior hits the pause button while he talks on the phone, negotiating a sleep-over with a friend he met in advanced kindergym. Meanwhile, Mum is thrashing through an aquafit aerobics class after work. But she has promised to be home in time to put Junior to bed and spend some quality time with Dad watching *thirtysomething*.

If the Sixties produced revolution and the Seventies belonged to the Me Generation, the Eighties were a time for consolidation. Ending an era of wishful thinking, it was the decade in which members of the baby-boom generation tried to find their way home. For years, they had been afraid of turning into their parents, of boring each other with talk of mortgage rates and the superi-ority of gas barbecues. But by the end of the 1970s, the alternatives had lost their appeal. The freedoms associated with sex, drugs and rock 'n' roll evaporated in the sobering light of a new decade. The AIDS epidemic cast a deadening pall over promiscuity. Cocaine, once the luxury drug of the discos, was reborn as the cheap contaminant called crack. The street became a scary place. Even Keith Richards, the Rolling Stones guitarist who endured a long romance with heroin, began behaving like a family man.

"Parenting" — suitable jargon for the functionalism of the era — became intensely fashion-able. As women watched their biological clocks wind down, the glamour of a career without children soon paled. The last holdouts finally began having babies, and they tried to do it on their own terms. Guided by the latest theories in feminist self-help, fast-track career women believed that they could expand their horizons without losing professional ground. They *had* the technology. After all, this was the modern age of day care and nannies — and sensitive men who claimed they were willing to share the load.

But it didn't work out the way it was supposed to. Women who had gone to all the trouble of having children began to wonder why they weren't spending any time with them. By the end of the decade, many mothers had traded in the dream of "having it all" for the concept of "the mommy track" — part-time corporate careers for working mothers. It was an idea that struck some feminists as heresy, but it indicated that the corporate world was only just beginning to grapple with a radical change in family structures. The two-career household was still an unproven prototype, prone to stress. There were no commonly accepted ground rules. When a sick child had to stay home, parents had to decide whose work should suffer.

The decade became a prolonged lesson in responsibility. One of the top-grossing movies, *Three Men and a Baby*, presented a comic fable about bachelors who slip out of the fast lane and become doting fathers. And the vastly popular *Fatal Attraction*, a cautionary thriller about the perils of adultery, typified a mounting preoccupation with monogamy and family values. Meanwhile, television viewers witnessed a gradual progression toward shows designed to mimic the lives of those watching them. In 1980, TV's most pressing question was "Who killed J. R. Ewing?" By 1989 prime time's hottest soap, *thirtysomething*, was posing questions a little more profound: Could Michael and Hope afford a second child? How could Nancy take all the credit for writing a children's book based on a bedtime story created by her estranged husband, Elliot? Some

For families in the Eighties, time became the ultimate luxury.

viewers complained about the show's whining tone. Its characters acted as if they were the first people in history to have children. But the dilemma of two-career couples—in an economy that offered little choice—*was* a relatively new development. And *thirtysomething* mirrored its viewers' anxieties with painful accuracy.

The 1980s was the decade that coined the regrettable catchword "yuppie." And *thirtysomething* was a part of an explosion of consumer marketing aimed at a new generation of style-conscious parents. If they did not have enough time for their children, they certainly made up for it in child-care equipment and accessories. Designer clothing turned toddlers into fashion victims. The Italian-built Perego stroller became the BMW of infant transport. Children's fantasies were horizontally integrated, with TV cartoons creating versatile armies of monsters and robots that reappeared as toys, costumes, games and sugar-coated cereal.

Technology shrank the world down to household scale. Personal computers, video cassettes and compact discs created new reasons not to go out. And with soaring real estate prices, the house itself became the ultimate consumer fetish. In the same decade that the homeless received charitable recognition, home ownership slipped further out of reach for those born too late or too poor. For the affluent, the home became a crossroads of enterprise. Individuals who once prided themselves on low-rent self-sufficiency suddenly found themselves employing a network of nannies, cleaning ladies and contractors. No wonder they found solace in small victories—the simplicity of a sun deck, the brilliance of a skylight.

By the dawn of the 1990s, the nuclear family had mutated into a makeshift organism with a short half-life. But the soaring divorce rate no longer seemed so alarming. Family structures had learned to tolerate separation. With shared custody, some parents had at least worked out equitable schedules of child care that eluded them in marriage. A child living with both biological parents may even have had reason to envy friends who commuted, like little cosmopolitans, between divorced parents. They could draw on an extended family, and two sets of toys.

In the 1980s, the postnuclear family acquired a measure of resilience. As it searched for stability and consumer satisfaction, there were echoes of the 1950s, flashbacks to the decade when *thirtysomething* parents were growing up. The suburban innocence of that era was gone forever. But in the no-man's land between marriage and divorce and on the reclaimed ground between home and work, a new kind of family was taking root.   —BRIAN D. JOHNSON

248

Dinosaurs were given new life in the late 1980s when moviemakers, television animators, gift manufacturers and even museums capitalized on the popular obsession with the extinct creatures.

OPPOSITE:
There were Wrinkles puppets, Strawberry Shortcakes and even Teenage Mutant Ninja Turtles. But no toy craze matched that of the Cabbage Patch Kids, round-faced munchkins who came with birth certificates and adoption papers — and spent little time on the shelf.

PUBLIC LIVES

Hers was the most famous — and the most photographed — face of the decade. The former Diana Spencer matured into a self-assured princess, a devoted mother and a trendsetter without equal. Grinning or pouting, pregnant or model-thin, she was the darling of the international press.

In a 1980 photograph that shocked Britons, a shy nineteen-year-old Lady Diana Spencer — then dating Prince Charles — was captured in a light summer skirt at a south London kindergarten where she worked part time.

BELOW:
When Princess Anne was married, she announced that she did not want "yards of uncontrollable children." Lady Diana Spencer, on the other hand, chose seven youngsters for her wedding party, including Clementine Hambro, her favorite pupil. The July, 1981, wedding provoked an explosion of popular — and private — emotion.

ABOVE LEFT:
Passionate about fashion, the lean and elegant princess became a leader in style.

ABOVE:
Britain's royal women at a Remembrance Day service in 1987: Diana, Princess of Wales, Princess Anne, the Duchess of York, and the Queen Mother.

LEFT:
An avid fan of rock 'n' roll, Diana greeted Mike Reno of the Canadian group Loverboy at the gala rock concert of Vancouver's Expo 86.

More than half a million spectators lined the streets of London on July 23, 1986, to celebrate the wedding of royal playboy Prince Andrew — nicknamed Randy Andy — and the vivacious Sarah (Fergie) Ferguson. "I want everyone to have a wonderful time," announced the future Duchess of York. And for the rest of the decade, the spirited couple tried to do just that — despite public censure. In 1988 Sarah was severely criticized for her decision to leave her seven-week-old daughter, Beatrice, at home while she joined Andrew in Australia for a six-week tour.

It was Canada's version of a royal wedding: in July, 1988, hockey superstar Wayne Gretzky married American actress Janet Jones.

Television actress Robin Givens proved that she, too, could get out of a tight corner. With her tumultuous, one-year marriage to heavyweight boxing champ Mike Tyson on the rocks in 1988, Givens filed for divorce — and a fifty-fifty asset split. Tyson called her ''slime.'' Givens duly responded with an enormous libel suit.

OPPOSITE:
Actor Sylvester Stallone and statuesque model Brigitte Nielsen spent much of their time together working out. But less than two years after their marriage in 1985, they parted in a well-publicized divorce. Nielsen — reportedly $7.8 million richer — moved on to New York Jets star Mark Gastineau.

ABOVE:
In 1981 actor Richard Thomas won the real-life role of father to triplet daughters.

RIGHT:
Scruffy rock 'n' roll star Billy Joel married his uptown girl, supermodel Christie Brinkley, who gave birth to Alexa Ray in 1986.

BELOW:
As far as the tabloids were concerned, the love life of actress Jessica Lange was more engrossing than her performances in *Frances*, *Sweet Dreams* and *Tootsie*. The Oscar-winner was attached to two of the most eligible men of the Eighties: dancer Mikhail Baryshnikov, father of her daughter, Aleksandra, and actor/ playwright Sam Shepard, her co-star in *Frances*, with whom she had two more children.

Unlike his companion, actress Mia Farrow — who already had eight children, five of whom were adopted — film-maker Woody Allen vowed that he did not ''care about heirs.'' But that changed after Farrow gave birth to his son, Satchel, in 1987.

BELOW:
When Margaret Kemper and her second husband, Ottawa real estate agent Fried Kemper, announced the birth of their first child in 1984, the gender came as no surprise: like the three children by Mrs. Kemper's former husband, Pierre Trudeau, the baby was a boy, Kyle (*shown here*). But in 1989 Kemper changed her habits, giving birth to her first daughter, Alicia Mary Rose.

SPECTACLES AND CELEBRATIONS

On the July Fourth weekend in 1986, Americans celebrated the centennial of the Statue of Liberty, newly restored at a cost of $97 million.

OPPOSITE:
Natives rowed Queen Elizabeth II ashore during her month-long 1982 tour of Papua New Guinea, Fiji and other small islands in the South Pacific, an exotic destination for the most-travelled monarch in history.

BELOW:

Vancouver provided a dramatic setting for the spectacular pavilions and plazas of Expo 86, including Expo Centre, a seventeen-storey geodesic dome. The six-month fair, attended by more than twenty-two million visitors, was one of the most popular of the decade.

RIGHT:

In their first official visit to Canada as the Duke and Duchess of York, Andrew and Sarah charmed onlookers with their energy and spontaneity in 1987, especially during a two-week canoe trip in the Northwest Territories.

OPPOSITE:
The surprise crowd-pleaser of the decade was Pope John Paul II. Despite his stern conservatism, the pontiff's 1984 Canadian tour drew the kind of clamorous welcome ordinarily reserved for rock stars.

Since its unveiling in 1982, the Vietnam Veterans Memorial in Washington, D.C., has drawn millions of friends and compatriots of the more than 50,000 U.S. war dead whose names are etched on its black granite wall — and on the American psyche.

Vicki Keith once described herself as "stark raving mad." But to millions the marathon swimmer was a hero for crossing the bone-chilling waters of all five Great Lakes in 1988, and in the process raising more than $500,000 for an aquatics centre for disabled children.

OPPOSITE:
It was one of the decade's greatest odysseys. Former Olympians Ferd Hayward and Barbara Ann Scott-King were the first of more than 6,000 to participate in the Olympic torch run, passing the flame, hand over hand, on its cross-Canada voyage to the 1988 Winter Games in Calgary.

FOLLOWING PAGES:
For sixteen nights in 1988, the Olympic torch blazed on the Calgary skyline.

CHRONOLOGY

JANUARY

14: Indira Gandhi re-elected prime minister of India.

14: UN General Assembly requests withdrawal of Soviet troops from Afghanistan.

22: Soviet dissident Andrei Sakharov exiled to Gorky.

29: Six U.S. Embassy officials, posing as Canadians, escape from Iran.

FEBRUARY

12: Opening of Lake Placid Winter Olympics.

22: Martial law declared in Afghanistan.

MARCH

3: Pierre Elliott Trudeau sworn in for his fourth term as prime minister of Canada.

24: Archbishop Oscar Romero assassinated in San Salvador.

27: North Sea oil platform collapses, killing 123.

APRIL

7: U.S. breaks diplomatic ties with Iran.

12: U.S. Olympic Committee votes to boycott Moscow Games.

18: Zimbabwe gains independence from British rule.

MAY

6: U.S. state of emergency declared as thousands of Cuban refugees enter Florida.

18: Mount St. Helens erupts.

20: Voters reject separatism in Quebec referendum.

JUNE

30: U.S. Supreme Court rules government is not constitutionally responsible to fund abortions.

JULY

1: "O Canada" proclaimed Canada's national anthem.

19: Widely boycotted Summer Olympics open in Moscow.

29: UN General Assembly approves resolution calling for formation of a Palestinian state.

AUGUST

11: Hurricane Allen leaves 270 dead in the Caribbean.

24: Labor unrest in Poland leads to massive strike of 200,000 workers.

SEPTEMBER

22: War begins between Iran and Iraq.

24: Poland's independent trade union Solidarity is registered in Warsaw court.

OCTOBER

10: Earthquake in Al Asnam, Algeria, kills an estimated 20,000.

22: China and Washington sign a bilateral grain agreement.

NOVEMBER

4: Ronald Reagan wins American election.

21: Fire at the MGM Grand Hotel in Las Vegas kills eighty-four.

23: Earthquake in southern Italy kills 3,000.

25: Sugar Ray Leonard defeats Roberto Durán, regaining welterweight boxing title.

DECEMBER

8: Former Beatle John Lennon murdered by Mark David Chapman.

13: José Napoleón Duarte named El Salvador's first civilian president in forty-nine years.

21: Washington refuses to pay Iran $24 billion (U.S.) for release of American hostages.

JANUARY

20: Ronald Reagan sworn in as U.S. president.

20: Fifty-two American hostages freed from Iran.

25: China's ''Gang of Four'' convicted of counterrevolutionary crimes.

FEBRUARY

9: General Wojciech Jaruzelski replaces Poland's Premier Josef Pinkowski.

24: Prince Charles announces engagement to Lady Diana Spencer.

MARCH

2: Washington sends $25 million in military aid to El Salvador.

11: General Augusto Pinochet declares himself president of Chile.

30: President Ronald Reagan shot and wounded in Washington.

30: Tentative labor agreement reached in Poland after 13 million strike in the name of Solidarity.

APRIL

13: Quebec's Parti Québécois re-elected.

MAY

5: IRA hunger striker Bobby Sands dies in Maze Prison, Belfast.

10: Socialist François Mitterrand elected president of France.

13: Turkish terrorist Ali Agca shoots Pope John Paul II.

30: Bangladesh President Ziaur Rahman slain.

JUNE

7: Israeli fighter planes destroy Osirak nuclear reactor in Iraq.

16: President Ferdinand Marcos re-elected in Philippines.

22: Ayatollah Ruhollah Khomeini dismisses Abolhassan Bani-Sadr as president of Iran.

JULY

4: John McEnroe defeats Bjorn Borg at Wimbledon.

7: Sandra Day O'Connor becomes first woman appointed to U.S. Supreme Court.

17: Israeli jets bomb Beirut, 300 die.

17: Two Hyatt Regency Hotel walkways in Kansas City collapse, 111 die.

29: Prince Charles weds Lady Diana Spencer.

31: Major league baseball ends seven-week strike.

AUGUST

10: Canadian Union of Postal Workers ends six-week strike.

25: *Voyager 2* transmits photos of planet Saturn.

30: Bomb kills Iranian President Mohammed Ali Rajai and Prime Minister Javad Bahonar.

SEPTEMBER

16: Polish Communist party denounces trade union Solidarity in strongest attack to date.

16: Sugar Ray Leonard wins world welterweight boxing title.

28: Canadian Supreme Court rules patriation of Constitution legal.

OCTOBER

6: Egyptian President Anwar Sadat assassinated.

18: Andreas Papandreou's Socialist party wins Greek elections.

NOVEMBER

5: Federal government and all provinces but Quebec reach compromise on patriating Canadian Constitution.

DECEMBER

13: Martial law declared in Poland.

JANUARY

12: Moscow and Washington resume negotiations on medium-range missiles.

28: U.S. Brigadier-General James Dozier rescued after being kidnapped by Italian Red Brigade terrorists.

FEBRUARY

5: Great Britain becomes first European member of NATO to impose sanctions against Poland.

MARCH

4: Bertha Wilson appointed first woman to Canadian Supreme Court.

15: Nicaragua's Sandinista government declares state of siege.

APRIL

2: Argentine troops seize the British-held Falkland Islands.

17: Queen Elizabeth II and Prime Minister Pierre Trudeau sign the Canadian Constitution Act.

30: Britain imposes air and sea blockade of Falkland Islands.

MAY

1: 1982 World's Fair opens in Knoxville, Tennessee.

2: Britain sinks Argentine cruiser, the *General Belgrano*, more than 360 die.

18: Reverend Sun Myung Moon found guilty of tax evasion.

29: Pope John Paul II becomes first pontiff to visit Britain.

JUNE

17: Argentine President Leopoldo Galtieri resigns after Falkland Islands defeat.

21: Princess Diana gives birth to a son, William.

26: Israeli forces invade southern Lebanon.

30: Proposed U.S. Equal Rights Amendment defeated.

JULY

20: IRA bomb kills nine soldiers in London.

AUGUST

19: Israel accepts plan to end Beirut siege; PLO begins pulling out.

SEPTEMBER

14: Lebanese President-elect Bashir Gemayel assassinated.

16: Christian Phalangists massacre Palestinians at Sabra and Shatila refugee camps.

OCTOBER

1: Christian Democrat Helmut Kohl elected chancellor of West Germany.

5: Tylenol recalled after seventh death from cyanide-laced capsules in Chicago area.

8: Polish parliament outlaws Solidarity.

19: Automobile executive John De Lorean charged with possession and conspiring to distribute cocaine.

NOVEMBER

5: More than 10,000 Canadian United Auto Workers strike.

12: Former KGB chief Yuri Andropov chosen general secretary of Soviet Communist party after Leonid Brezhnev dies.

14: Lech Walesa released after eleven months in prison.

DECEMBER

2: Barney Clark receives first permanent artificial heart.

13: Earthquake in Yemen Arab Republic kills more than 2,800.

31: Martial law partially lifted in Poland.

JANUARY

3: Officially sanctioned Polish trade unions replace outlawed Solidarity federation.

13: Israel and Lebanon agree to agenda for peace talks.

25: Former Gestapo boss Klaus Barbie arrested in Bolivia.

FEBRUARY

11: Israeli Defence Minister Ariel Sharon resigns.

21: Joint U.S.-Canada study fails to agree on causes and effects of acid rain.

MARCH

5: Robert Hawke elected prime minister of Australia.

23: President Ronald Reagan proposes Star Wars defence plan.

APRIL

9: Space shuttle *Challenger* completes first successful mission.

18: Car bomb explodes at U.S. Embassy in Beirut, killing seventy.

MAY

6: *The Hitler Diaries*, published in *Stern* magazine, are proved fraudulent.

20: South Africa's ANC bombs national air force headquarters in Pretoria, killing eighteen.

JUNE

9: Britain's Prime Minister Margaret Thatcher increases parliamentary majority in national election.

11: Brian Mulroney wins leadership of Canada's Progressive Conservative party.

18: Sally Ride becomes the first American woman in space.

23: Pope John Paul II ends visit to his native Poland.

JULY

13: British House of Commons rejects motion to restore death penalty.

21: End of martial law in Poland.

AUGUST

1: More than 200 killed in ethnic violence in Sri Lanka.

21: Philippine opposition leader Benigno Aquino assassinated.

SEPTEMBER

1: Soviet missile brings down Korean Air Lines Boeing 747, killing 269.

2: Yitzhak Shamir elected prime minister of Israel.

OCTOBER

5: Lech Walesa wins Nobel Peace Prize.

23: Terrorist assault on U.S. Marine headquarters in Beirut kills 241.

25: U.S. troops invade Grenada.

NOVEMBER

24: Israel releases 4,500 Palestinian and Lebanese prisoners for return of six captured soldiers.

DECEMBER

8: Strategic Arms Reduction Talks between Washington and U.S.S.R. end in stalemate.

15: South Africa announces withdrawal of troops from southern Angola.

26: Japanese Prime Minister Yasuhiro Nakasone elected to second term.

JANUARY

6: Statistics Canada reports nation's unemployment rate highest since 1936, at 11.9 per cent.

FEBRUARY

8: The XIV Winter Olympics begin in Yugoslavia.

10: China and the U.S.S.R. sign $1.2-billion trade agreement.

13: Konstantin Chernenko becomes Soviet leader when Yuri Andropov dies after only fifteen months in office.

26: Canadian Prime Minister Pierre Trudeau announces resignation.

29: U.S. Marines leave Lebanon.

MARCH

16: South Africa and Mozambique sign historic nonaggression treaty.

21: Canada signs acid rain agreement with nine European nations.

APRIL

15: The Tall Ships begin retracing Jacques Cartier's voyage.

MAY

7: Soviets announce boycott of Los Angeles Summer Olympics.

8: Gunman opens fire in Quebec National Assembly, killing three.

11: José Napoleón Duarte wins presidency of El Salvador.

14: Jeanne Sauvé becomes Canada's first woman governor general.

19: Edmonton Oilers win their first Stanley Cup.

JUNE

17: John Turner elected leader of Canada's Liberal party.

30: John Turner becomes prime minister of Canada.

JULY

19: Geraldine Ferraro becomes first woman to run for U.S. vice president.

28: The Los Angeles Summer Olympics begin.

SEPTEMBER

4: Brian Mulroney elected prime minister of Canada.

5: Space shuttle *Discovery* completes successful maiden flight.

6: Typhoon Ike kills 1,400 in southern Philippines.

9: Pope John Paul II begins first tour of Canada.

OCTOBER

2: Three Soviet cosmonauts complete longest space mission: 237 days.

12: British Prime Minister Margaret Thatcher and cabinet members escape IRA bomb in Brighton hotel.

16: Bishop Desmond Tutu wins Nobel Peace Prize.

31: India's Indira Gandhi killed by Sikh bodyguards.

NOVEMBER

6: President Ronald Reagan returned to office.

6: Violence and national strike force Chile to declare state of siege.

15: Baby Fae dies after twenty days with baboon heart.

26: Washington and Iraq restore diplomatic ties.

DECEMBER

3: Toxic gas leak from Union Carbide plant in Bhopal, India, leaves 2,500 dead.

25: Vietnamese troops mount major attack against rebel camps on Cambodian border.

29: Rajiv Gandhi elected prime minister of India.

JANUARY

19: Parti Québécois rejects independence as an option.

FEBRUARY

3: Desmond Tutu becomes first black Anglican bishop of Johannesburg.

8: Opposition leader Kim Dae Jung returns to South Korea after exile.

MARCH

3: End of British coal miners' year-long strike.

11: Mikhail Gorbachev elected new leader of Soviet Union.

12: Three Armenian terrorists seize Turkish Embassy in Ottawa, killing a guard.

17: Shamrock Summit begins in Quebec City.

21: South African police kill nineteen blacks in Uitenhage.

APRIL

7: Gorbachev freezes intermediate nuclear missile deployment.

MAY

1: President Ronald Reagan orders trade embargo with Nicaragua.

20: Israel exchanges 1,150 Arab prisoners for three Israeli soldiers.

25: A cyclone and tidal wave kill up to 10,000 in Bangladesh.

29: Soccer fans riot in Brussels, thirty-eight die.

29: Steve Fonyo, one-legged cancer victim, ends cross-Canada run.

31: Tornado in Barrie, Ontario, kills twelve.

JUNE

14: TWA Flight 847 hijacked en route from Cairo to Rome.

23: Terrorist bomb downs Air India jetliner near Ireland, killing 329.

30: Hijackers release remaining hostages on TWA Flight 847.

JULY

10: Bomb planted by French agents sinks Greenpeace's *Rainbow Warrior* in Auckland harbor.

13: Live Aid concerts raise $95 million for African famine relief.

20: South Africa declares first state of emergency in twenty-five years.

AUGUST

12: Japan Air Lines crash near Tokyo kills 520.

SEPTEMBER

19: An earthquake in Mexico erupts over a two-day period, leaving an estimated 25,000 dead.

23: Canadian Fisheries Minister John Fraser resigns over ''tainted tuna'' scandal.

OCTOBER

1: Israeli planes bomb PLO headquarters in Tunis, seventy-three killed.

5: Toronto Blue Jays win first divisional championship.

7: Palestinian terrorists hijack Italian cruise ship *Achille Lauro*.

NOVEMBER

13: Colombian volcano Nevado del Ruiz erupts twice, killing more than 23,000.

15: Anglo-Irish accord reached, giving Irish Republic formal say in governing Northern Ireland.

19: Ronald Reagan and Mikhail Gorbachev meet in Geneva for first U.S.-Soviet summit in six years.

DECEMBER

12: Air crash in Gander, Newfoundland, kills 248 American soldiers and eight crew.

27: Palestinian terrorists bomb Rome and Vienna airports, killing eighteen.

1986

JANUARY

7: President Ronald Reagan cuts economic ties with Libya.

16: Fourth round of U.S.-Soviet arms talks open in Geneva.

23: United States begins manoeuvres off Libyan coast.

28: Space shuttle *Challenger* explodes, killing seven astronauts.

FEBRUARY

7: Haiti's president-for-life, Jean-Claude Duvalier, flees for France after antigovernment protests.

8: Train collision near Hinton, Alberta, kills twenty-six.

26: Corazon Aquino recognized as Philippine president.

28: Sweden's Prime Minister Olof Palme assassinated.

MARCH

20: Jacques Chirac assumes office as French prime minister.

23: U.S. and Libyan forces clash off Libyan coast.

APRIL

14: Americans bomb Libyan military targets and home of Colonel Moammar Gadhafi.

26: Explosion at Chernobyl nuclear power station in Soviet Union dangerously exposes citizens to radiation.

MAY

1: South Africa hit by strike as 1.5 million blacks stay off their jobs.

2: Expo 86 opens in Vancouver.

11: Sinclair Stevens, federal minister of regional industrial expansion, resigns in a conflict-of-interest scandal.

19: South African forces attack Botswana, Zimbabwe and Zambia.

JUNE

8: Despite charges of Nazi activity, Kurt Waldheim elected president of Austria.

25: House of Representatives approves $100 million (U.S.) to Nicaraguan contra rebels.

JULY

23: Prince Andrew weds Sarah Ferguson.

AUGUST

5: Britain's Prime Minister Margaret Thatcher agrees to limited sanctions against South Africa.

6: Longest-surviving artificial heart recipient, William J. Schroeder, dies, 620 days after surgery.

21: Poisonous gas emissions from volcanic lake in Cameroon kill 1,700.

SEPTEMBER

8: Pakistani opposition leader Benazir Bhutto, released after twenty-five days in prison.

OCTOBER

12: U.S. and Soviet leaders end Reykjavik arms summit in stalemate.

NOVEMBER

25: U.S. Attorney General Edwin Meese reports profits from arms sales to Iran were diverted to Nicaraguan contras.

30: John Turner wins strong support as Liberal party leader during an Ottawa convention.

DECEMBER

23: *Voyager*, an experimental U.S. plane, completes first nonstop flight around the world without refuelling.

JANUARY

9: Iran launches major offensive against Iraq, one of the bloodiest in the six-year war.

20: Anglican Church envoy Terry Waite disappears in Lebanon while seeking Western hostages.

FEBRUARY

9: Former U.S. national security adviser Robert McFarlane, a key figure in Iran-contra affair, attempts suicide.

MARCH

6: British ferry capsizes off coast of Belgium, 188 die.

19: Jim Bakker resigns from PTL ministry after admitting adultery.

APRIL

21: Attack by Tamil rebels leaves hundreds dead in Sri Lanka.

MAY

5: Washington opens public hearings in Iran-contra scandal.

6: Whites-only vote returns South Africa's P. W. Botha to power.

8: U.S. presidential candidate Gary Hart withdraws following reports of extramarital indiscretion.

17: USS *Stark* is hit by Iraqi missiles, killing thirty-seven.

29: West German pilot Mathias Rust lands plane in Moscow's Red Square.

JUNE

3: Quebec accepts the 1982 Constitution after signing the Meech Lake accord.

18: Rioting students battle police in Seoul.

JULY

4: Former Nazi Klaus Barbie receives life sentence in France.

31: Tornado in Edmonton area kills twenty-seven.

AUGUST

24: Soviet spy, U.S. Marine Sergeant Clayton Lonetree, sentenced to thirty years.

SEPTEMBER

4: Mathias Rust sentenced to four years in Soviet labor camp.

4: Weeks of flooding in Bangladesh leave 24 million homeless.

15: Team Canada defeats Soviet Union in Canada Cup hockey.

OCTOBER

3: Ottawa and Washington reach free trade agreement.

11: Libya and Chad agree to ceasefire in border war.

16: After a two-day ordeal, baby Jessica McClure is rescued from a Texas well shaft.

19: Black Monday stock market crash drives the Dow Jones average down by 508 points.

NOVEMBER

11: Vincent van Gogh's *Irises* sells for a record $71.5 million.
17: Fire in London subway kills thirty.

29: Haiti's first attempted free elections in thirty years spark violence, killing thirty-four.

DECEMBER

8: Washington and Moscow sign treaty eliminating intermediate-range nuclear missiles.

9: Massive fighting breaks out between Palestinians and Israelis in West Bank, Gaza Strip, seventeen die.

20: Ferry and oil tanker collide off the Philippines, killing 1,600.

1988

JANUARY

2: Prime Minister Brian Mulroney signs Free Trade Agreement.

26: Two million gather in Sydney to begin celebration of Australian bicentennial.

FEBRUARY

5: Panamanian dictator General Manuel Noriega indicted in Miami for drug smuggling.

13: Opening of the Calgary Olympics.

28: Ethnic rioting in Soviet Azerbaijan kills more than thirty.

MARCH

16: Iraq launches chemical gas attack on Kurdish village, killing thousands.

16: Protestant gunman kills three at IRA funeral in Belfast.

19: Two British soldiers killed during Belfast funeral procession.

23: Sandinistas and contras agree to a ceasefire in Nicaragua.

APRIL

18: Former Nazi John Demjanjuk is convicted in Israel of war crimes.

MAY

8: François Mitterrand re-elected as French president.

15: Soviets begin Afghanistan withdrawal.

26: Vietnam announces withdrawal from Cambodia.

29: President Ronald Reagan begins first Soviet visit.

JUNE

8: Two million black workers end three-day strike in South Africa.

28: Opening of first Soviet Communist party conference since 1941.

JULY

3: U.S. warship downs Iranian airbus over Persian Gulf, 290 die.

6: North Sea explosion on Piper Alpha oil platform kills 166.

18: Iran agrees to end war with Iraq.

AUGUST

17: Pakistani leader Zia ul-Haq dies in plane explosion.

23: Demonstrators in three Baltic capitals oppose Soviet rule.

SEPTEMBER

6: Official death toll rises to 490 in Bangladesh floods.

12: Hurricane Gilbert hits Jamaica, leaving 500,000 homeless.

17: Opening of Seoul Olympics.

22: Canada announces compensation for Japanese-Canadians interned during Second World War.

27: Ben Johnson stripped of Olympic gold medal.

OCTOBER

5: Chilean President Augusto Pinochet defeated in plebiscite.

NOVEMBER

8: George Bush wins U.S. election.

15: PLO proclaims Palestinian state.

16: Estonia claims right to veto Soviet laws.

21: Prime Minister Brian Mulroney re-elected.

DECEMBER

1: Pakistan's Benazir Bhutto becomes first woman prime minister of Moslem state.

7: Mikhail Gorbachev pledges 10-per-cent reduction in Soviet conventional armed forces.

7: Earthquake strikes Armenia, killing 55,000.

14: Washington announces first talks with PLO since relations banned.

15: Supreme Court of Canada strikes down a controversial section of Quebec language law.

21: Air crash in Scotland kills 270.

22: South Africa, Angola and Cuba sign agreement on Namibian independence.

JANUARY

1: U.S.–Canada Free Trade Agreement takes effect.

1: Celebration of the French Revolution bicentennial begins.

4: U.S. navy fighters down two Libyan jets.

11: Opening of the Dubin inquiry into the use of drugs in amateur sports.

15: Bangladesh train crash kills at least 170.

20: George Bush sworn in as U.S. president.

22: Newfoundland Premier Brian Peckford announces his resignation.

31: Oliver North's trial begins in Washington.

FEBRUARY

3: Alfredo Stroessner's rule of Paraguay ends in a military coup.

14: Ayatollah Ruhollah Khomeini condemns Salman Rushdie's *The Satanic Verses*.

15: Soviet withdrawal from Afghanistan completed.

16: South African Winnie Mandela is denounced for use of tough bodyguards.

28: Martial law is declared in Venezuela; 300 die in riots.

MARCH

2: The European Community agrees to phase out the production of chlorofluorocarbons by the year 2000.

4: Ed Broadbent resigns as leader of the national New Democratic Party.

4: Time Inc. and Warner Communications agree to merge, forming the world's largest media and entertainment group.

19: Alfredo Cristiani, of the right-wing Nationalist Republican Alliance (ARENA), wins the presidency of El Salvador.

23: Scientists Martin Fleischmann and Stanley Pons announce discovery of a controlled nuclear fusion reaction at room temperature, which later was challenged.

24: The *Exxon Valdez* runs aground in the Gulf of Alaska, spilling 240,000 barrels of oil.

26: The Soviet Union holds its first multicandidate general election since 1917.

APRIL

16: Pro-democracy demonstrations begin in China.

25: Japanese Premier Noboru Takeshita resigns during Recruit scandal.

26: The Canadian federal budget is leaked.

MAY

3: John Turner resigns as leader of the national Liberal party.

10: Strongman General Manuel Noriega declares Panama elections void, remains in control, inciting violence.

15: Mikhail Gorbachev arrives in Beijing for historic Sino-Soviet summit.

17: One million students occupy Beijing's Tiananmen Square.

JUNE

4: Chinese troops massacre civilians in Tiananmen Square.

4: Ali Khamenei named successor to Ayatollah Khomeini, one day after the death of Iran's spiritual leader.

18: In final round of elections, Solidarity candidates gain all 161 seats permitted to opposition members in Polish legislature.

21: First executions of the Tiananmen Square protesters in Shanghai.

JULY

14: Coal miners strike in Siberia and the Ukraine, causing one of the worst labor disturbances in Soviet history.

24: After two months in office, Japanese Prime Minister Sousuke Uno resigns.

PASSAGES

Alfred Hitchcock (1899–1980)

Mohammed Reza Pahlavi (1919–1980)

1980

Jimmy Durante, mirthful star of vaudeville and television.

Alfred Hitchcock, master of cinematic suspense.

Alexei Kosygin, Soviet premier (1964–1980).

Judy LaMarsh, former Liberal cabinet minister, author and social reformer.

Jules Léger, former governor general of Canada.

John Lennon, brilliant musician, composer and poet of Beatles fame.

Jean Lesage, leader of the Quiet Revolution, Quebec premier (1960–1966).

Marshall McLuhan, controversial Canadian thinker famous for his statement: ''The medium is the message.''

Steve McQueen, blue-eyed, macho movie star.

Henry Miller, infamous American author of *Tropic of Cancer*.

Jesse Owens, black track-and-field star of 1936 Olympics.

Mohammed Reza Pahlavi, exiled shah of Iran.

Jean Piaget, Swiss psychologist and educator.

Jean-Paul Sartre, existentialist philosopher.

Peter Sellers, comedic chameleon beloved as the bumbling Inspector Clouseau.

Anastosio Somoza Debayle, former Nicara-guan strongman.

Josip Broz Tito, former Yugoslavian leader who defied Stalin.

Mae West, lusty movie star of the Thirties and Forties.

1981

Thérèse Casgrain, Canadian politician, author and civil libertarian.

Moshe Dayan, Israeli soldier-statesman.

Frédéric Dorion, chief justice of the Quebec Superior Court who led an inquiry into federal corruption during the Pearson years.

Melvyn Douglas, powerful character actor (*Hud, Being There*).

Will and Ariel Durant, co-authors of *The Story of Civilization*.

Terry Fox, courageous one-legged runner who raised millions for cancer research.

Chief Dan George, chief of British Columbia's Tse-lal-watt tribe who won acclaim for his role in *Little Big Man*.

William Holden, Oscar-winning actor, star of *Sunset Boulevard*.

David Lewis, brilliant labor lawyer and father of New Democratic Party.

Joe Louis, heavyweight champion from 1937 to 1949.

Bob Marley, Jamaica's king of reggae music.

Anwar Sadat, Egyptian president awarded a Nobel Prize for his peace initiatives.

Albert Speer, Nazi minister of armaments who served twenty years in jail for war crimes.

Omar Torrijos Herrera, Panamanian dictator.

Natalie Wood, dark-eyed movie star (*Splendor in the Grass*).

Stefan Cardinal Wyszynski, Roman Catholic primate of Poland.

John Cheever (1912-1982)

Leonid Brezhnev (1906-1982)

Glenn Gould (1932-1982)

1982

John Belushi, manic star of *Saturday Night Live* and *Animal House*.

Ingrid Bergman, the beautiful and gifted Swedish-born star of *Casablanca* and *Gaslight*.

Leonid Brezhnev, Soviet leader from 1964 to 1982.

John Cheever, American literary genius (*Falconer*).

Rainer Werner Fassbinder, controversial West German film director of *The Marriage of Maria Braun*.

Henry Fonda, quintessential American film hero, remembered for his role in *The Grapes of Wrath*.

Glenn Gould, brilliant, provocative Toronto-born pianist.

Igor Gouzenko, Soviet Embassy clerk who defected to Canada with detailed evidence of his country's spy activities.

Grace Kelly, serenely beautiful star of *Rear Window* who married Monaco's Prince Rainier.

Thelonious Monk, bop jazz pianist.

Leroy (Satchel) Paige, legendary black American pitcher.

Ayn Rand, popular objectivist author of *The Fountainhead*.

Hans Selye, the "stress doctor," explorer of the mind-body connection.

Lee Strasberg, master of the "Method" school of acting.

Gilles Villeneuve, Canadian racing driver.

1983

Benigno Aquino, Jr., Philippine opposition leader, assassinated.

George Balanchine, influential dance choreographer.

Maurice Bishop, prime minister of Grenada, shot during a coup.

Anthony Blunt, British art historian accused of spying for the Soviets.

Karen Carpenter, American singer whose death followed a battle with anorexia nervosa.

Barney Clark, first recipient of a permanent artificial heart.

Sir Kenneth Clark, distinguished British art historian, author and narrator of BBC's *Civilisation*.

Jack Dempsey, the greatest boxer of his generation.

Richard Buckminster Fuller, American futuristic designer, developer of the geodesic dome.

Ira Gershwin, American lyricist, co-creator of *Porgy and Bess*.

Arthur Koestler, Hungarian-born author of *Darkness at Noon*.

Raymond Massey, versatile Canadian stage, film and television actor.

David Niven, urbane British actor (*Separate Tables*) and best-selling author.

Albert Rauca, German-Canadian immigrant extradited to West Germany on charges of Nazi war crimes.

Sir Ralph Richardson, one of Britain's most distinguished and beloved performers.

Gabrielle Roy, Canadian author of *The Tin Flute*.

Gloria Swanson, American actress, memorable for *Sunset Boulevard*.

John Vorster, South African prime minister from 1966 to 1978.

Rebecca West, British author, critic and feminist.

Tennessee Williams, American playwright (*A Streetcar Named Desire*, *Cat on a Hot Tin Roof*).

Truman Capote (1924-1984)

Richard Burton (1925-1984)

Marian Engel (1934-1985)

T.C. (Tommy) Douglas (1920-1986)

Olof Palme (1927-1986)

1984

Ansel Adams, photographer of heroic, luminous images of the American West.

Yuri Andropov, former head of the KGB and Soviet leader.

William (Count) Basie, legendary figure of the Big Band era.

Richard Burton, Welsh actor, renowned for his tempestuous private life.

Clarence Campbell, former president of the National Hockey League.

Truman Capote, flamboyant American author (*In Cold Blood*).

James Fixx, American guru of jogging.

George Gallup, American pioneer of polling.

Indira Gandhi, imperious prime minister of India.

Marvin Gaye, soulful Motown singer of classic rhythm and blues.

Lillian Hellman, controversial American author and dramatist (*The Little Foxes*).

Bora Laskin, chief justice of the Supreme Court of Canada.

James Mason, British actor, memorable as Judy Garland's husband in *A Star Is Born*.

Ethel Merman, brassy American star of stage and screen.

John Rock, developer of the birth control pill.

Mikhail Sholokhov, Soviet author (*And Quiet Flows the Don*).

Gordon Sinclair, gruff Toronto journalist and broadcaster.

François Truffaut, pioneering French film director (*Jules et Jim*).

1985

Hal C. Banks, iron-fisted union boss of the Canadian waterfront.

Yul Brynner, exotic star of *The King and I*.

Marc Chagall, Russian-born painter of a dreamlike, romantic world.

Konstantin Chernenko, Soviet leader for thirteen months.

Marian Engel, Toronto author and Governor General's Award winner for the controversial *Bear*.

Rock Hudson, one of Hollywood's most popular leading men, who disclosed that he had AIDS.

Ricky Nelson, former TV star and pop idol of the Fifties and Sixties.

Karen Ann Quinlan, subject of a precedent-setting, successful right-to-die appeal filed by her parents after she fell into a coma.

Sir Michael Redgrave, widely acclaimed British film and stage actor.

Francis Reginald (F. R.) Scott, influential Canadian poet, dean of law and moving spirit of the CCF.

Simone Signoret, French actress and Oscar winner (*Room at the Top*).

Samantha Smith, American student who visited the Soviet Union after writing to Yuri Andropov.

Orson Welles, gifted American actor, writer and director (*Citizen Kane*).

Elwyn Brooks (E. B.) White, essayist, poet and author of children's books (*Charlotte's Web*).

Margaret Laurence (1927-1987)

Fred Astaire (1899-1987)

Andy Warhol (1928-1987)

1986

Desi Arnaz, hot-blooded co-star of *I Love Lucy*.

Jorge Luis Borges, brilliant Argentine storyteller.

James Cagney, pugnacious American screen star.

Simone de Beauvoir, influential French writer and feminist (*The Second Sex*).

T. C. (Tommy) Douglas, veteran Canadian socialist and parliamentarian.

Benny Goodman, American bandleader and "King of Swing."

Cary Grant, debonair Hollywood star of more than seventy movies.

Don Jamieson, Newfoundland cabinet minister under Pierre Trudeau.

Alan Jay Lerner, co-creator of *Camelot*, *My Fair Lady* and *Gigi*.

Henry Moore, the most celebrated sculptor of the century.

Georgia O'Keeffe, innovative American painter of highly sensual, resonant images.

Olof Palme, Sweden's popular Socialist prime minister, assassinated.

Wallis Warfield Simpson, Duchess of Windsor, Baltimore divorcée, for whom King Edward VIII abdicated his throne.

1987

Fred Astaire, dapper actor and fluid dance partner of Ginger Rogers.

Jackie Gleason, the loudmouthed Ralph Kramden in *The Honeymooners*, Minnesota Fats in *The Hustler*.

Walter Gordon, social reformer and ardent nationalist.

Lorne Greene, pioneer of Canadian broadcasting, known to millions as Ben Cartwright on *Bonanza*.

Rita Hayworth, Hollywood's "Love Goddess."

Rudolf Hess, Adolf Hitler's deputy, sole inmate of Berlin's Spandau prison for twenty-one years.

John Huston, American director of *The Maltese Falcon* and *The Treasure of Sierra Madre*.

Danny Kaye, rubber-faced comedian of stage and screen.

Margaret Laurence, Canadian novelist, world-renowned for *The Stone Angel* and *The Diviners*.

René Lévesque, charter leader of the Parti Québécois and reformist Quebec premier from 1976 to 1985.

Geraldine Page, gifted actress of stage and screen.

Andrés Segovia, Spanish classical guitarist.

Andy Warhol, the most famous pop artist of the Sixties, whose image was as publicized as his art.

1988

Jean Gascon, former director of Stratford Festival, head of theatre at the National Arts Centre.

Andy Gibb, pop star.

George Grant, Canadian philosopher and author of *Lament for a Nation*.

Robert A. Heinlein, science fiction writer (*Stranger in a Strange Land*).

Emperor Hirohito (1902-1989)

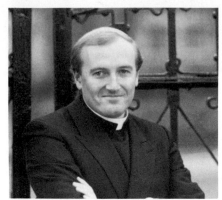

Sean O'Sullivan (1952–1989)

Lucille Ball (1912–1989)

John Houseman, producer, director and actor (*The Paper Chase*).

Trevor Howard, handsome male lead of *Mutiny on the Bounty* and *Brief Encounter*.

Arthur Lower, Canadian historian and author of the classic text *Colony to Nation: A History of Canada*.

Jean Marchand, former Quebec labor leader, federal cabinet minister and Speaker of the Senate who helped Pierre Trudeau in the fight against Quebec separatism.

Christina Onassis, multimillion-dollar heiress.

Roy Orbison, singer and songwriter of "Pretty Woman" fame.

Alan Paton, South African novelist whose *Cry, the Beloved Country* explored the tragedy of apartheid.

Harold (Kim) Philby, British double agent who fled to the Soviet Union to avoid being charged as a Communist spy.

Mohammed Zia ul-Haq, Pakistani president killed in airplane explosion.

1989

Lucille Ball, beloved star of *I Love Lucy*.

Donald Brittain, master Canadian film-maker, internationally renowned for brilliant documentaries and docudramas, including *The King Chronicle*.

John Cassavetes, American actor and director (*A Woman under the Influence*).

Bruce Chatwin, British novelist and travel writer (*In Patagonia*).

Malcolm Cowley, American poet, journalist, editor and chronicler of the 1920s literary scene.

Daphne du Maurier, British novelist whose suspenseful tales (*Rebecca, The Birds*) made it to the movies.

Emperor Hirohito, Japanese sovereign who had occupied the Chrysanthemum Throne since 1926.

John Hirsch, influential Canadian theatre director who oversaw the Stratford Festival from 1980 to 1985.

Abbie Hoffman, anti-establishment hero of the Sixties, one of the Chicago Seven.

Christine Jorgensen, famous recipient of a sex-change operation.

Sergio Leone, Italian film director and father of the spaghetti western.

Beatrice Lillie, Toronto-born actress, whom Noël Coward called the world's funniest woman.

Konrad Lorenz, Nobel Prize–winning Austrian zoologist and author of *On Aggression*.

Laurence Olivier, considered by many the greatest actor of the century, memorable for his magnificent performances on stage and screen (*Wuthering Heights, Hamlet*).

Sean O'Sullivan, former Canadian MP and assistant to John Diefenbaker, who left politics for the priesthood.

Gilda Radner, wacky comic of *Saturday Night Live* fame.

Merle Shain, Canadian writer (*Some Men Are More Perfect Than Others*).

Sir William Stephenson, Canadian master spy, whom Winston Churchill named "Intrepid."

Edward Plunkett (E. P.) Taylor, Canadian tycoon and race horse breeder.

Barbara Tuchman, famous American historian and author (*The Guns of August*).

PHOTO CREDITS

2: Brian Willer; 6–7: Publiphoto/Bisson/ Sygma; 8: Pono Presse International/ Gamma/Pool-Hires/Guerrini; 9 left: Canapresse/Fred Chartrand; right: Paul Hosefros/The New York Times; 10 top: David Turnley/Blackstar; 11: Sisson/SIPA; 12: Pono Presse Int./Gamma-Liaison/Brad Markel; 13 top: Pono Presse Int./Gamma; 14: Publiphoto/D. Aubert/ Sygma; 15 top: Pono Presse Int./Rex Features; bottom: Pono Presse Int./Gamma; 16 top and bottom: Reagan Presidential Materials Project; 17 top: Reuters/Bettman Newsphotos; bottom: Canada Wide; 18 top: Canapress; bottom: Canapress/Ray Giguere; 19: Neal Preston; 20: Derek Hudson/Sygma; 21 top: Canapress; bottom: Gail Harvey; 22 top: James Nachtwey/Magnum Photos; bottom: J. Langevin/Sygma; 23: Duomo; 24: Pono Presse Int./Gamma-Liaison; 25 top: Publiphoto/Dr. Robert Gale/ Sygma; 25 top: Publiphoto/Dr. Robert Gale/ Sygma; bottom: Publiphoto/Sygma; 26: Brian Willer; 27 top: A. Hernandez/Sygma; bottom: Publiphoto/Henri Bureau/Sygma; 28–29: Reagan Presidential Materials Project; 30: R. Nickelsberg/Gamma-Liaison: 31 top: Publiphoto/P. Robert/Sygma; bottom: Pono Presse Int./Gamma/Alain Mingam;32 top: Canapress/Michael Creagean; bottom: Mike Blake/Reuters/Bettman Newsphoto; 33: Pono Presse Int./Gamma-Liaison/Roland Neveu; 34: David Turnley/ Blackstar; 35 top: Pono Presse Int./Gamma/ Magubane-Liaison; bottom and 36–37: David Turnley/Blackstar; 39 top: Pono Presse Int./Gamma/Chip Hires; bottom: Publiphoto/P. Robert/Sygma; 40 top: Sven Simon; bottom: Publiphoto/Sygma; 41 top: Pono Presse Int./Gamma/An Nahar; bottom: Reuters/Bettman Newsphotos; 42: Morvan/SIPA; 43: Pono Presse Int./Gamma/ Pascal Maitre; 44: Gamma-Liaison; 45: Pono Presse Int./Gamma/ABC Ajansi; 46–47: Publiphoto/J. Pavlovsky/Sygma; 48 top: Reuters/Bettman Newsphotos; bottom: Canapress/Jeff Widener; 49 top: Publiphoto/A. Tannenbaum/Sygma; bottom: Pono Presse Int./Gamma/Chip Hires; 50: Kirck Halstead/Gamma-Liaison; 51 top: Pono Presse Int./Liaison/Johnson; bottom: Pono Presse Int./Gamma/Matthew Naythons; 52 top: Publiphoto/Manuel Ceniceras/Sygma; bottom and 53 top: UPI/ Bettman Newsphotos; 53 bottom: Ronald Reagan Presidential Materials Project; 54–55: Ron Haviv/AFP; 56 top: Pono Presse Int./

SIPA/Seiboon; bottom: Publiphoto/Jason Bleibtreu/Sygma; 57 top: Rosy Rouleau/ Sygma; bottom: Reuters/Bettman Newsphotos; 58 top and bottom: Brian Willer; 59: Graffoto/Armand Legault; 60 top: Canapress/Mitchell; 60 bottom: Brian Willer; 61 top left: Pam Price/Picture Group; top right: Canapress/Ron Poling; middle: Canapress; bottom: Bill McCarthy/PMO; 62: Publiphoto/ P. Kyrazis/Sygma; 63 left: Canapress/ Nancy Ackerman; 63 right: Publiphoto/B. Martin; 64 top: Canapress/Ron Poling; middle: Brian Willer; bottom: Canapress; 65: John Major; 66: Canapress/Vaughan; 67 and 68 top and bottom: Canapress; 69: Steve Simon/The Edmonton Journal; 70: Canapress; 71; Sygma; 72 top: J. Langevin/ Sygma; bottom: Canada Wide; 73 bottom: Canapress/Renate Flottau; 74–75: Pono Presse Int.; 76: Pono Presse Int./SIPA; 77: Pono Presse Int./Gamma/Kok; 78: Brian Willer; 79 top: Pono Presse Int./Rex Features; 79 bottom: Publiphoto/S. Franklin/ Sygma; 80–81: Rex Features; 81: Pono Presse Int./Gamma/François Lochon — Thierry Campion; 82: Pono Presse Int./ Gamma; 83: Publiphoto/D. Goldberg/ Sygma; 84 top: Pono Presse Int./Gamma/ Barry Iverson; bottom: Pono Presse Int./ Gamma/Nakram Gadel Karim — Al Akhbar; 85 top: Sandro Tucci/Gamma-Liaison; bottom: Publiphoto/Gianni Giansonti/Sygma; 86: Publiphoto/J.L. Atlan/Sygma; 87: Mark Woodbury & Associates/Canada Wide; 88 left: Publiphoto/R. Maiman/Sygma; right: UPI/Bettman Newsphotos; 89 left: Guy DeLort/Women's Wear Daily; right: Pono Presse Int./Rex Features; 90–91: Theo Westenberger/Sygma; 91: Pono Presse Int./ Gamma/Neveu; 92 left: Publiphoto/Tannenbaum/Sygma; top: Canapress/Ron Poling; bottom/right: Canapress; 93: Canapress/ Fred Chartrand; 94–95: Publiphoto/A. Nogues/Sygma; 95: AFP; 96 top: Publiphoto/Sygma; bottom: Greg Locke; 97 top: UPI/Bettman Newsphotos; bottom: Dan Scott/Vancouver Sun; 98–99: Pono Presse Int./Rex Features; 100: The Globe and Mail, Toronto; 101 left and right: Publiphoto/Helmut Newton/Sygma; 102: Publiphoto/ Sygma; 103: Bill Sanford/Canada Wide; 104 top left: Michael Creagen/Canada Wide; top right: UPI/Bettman Newsphotos; bottom: Canapress/Rick Loughran; 105 top: Fred Thornhill/Canada Wide; bottom: William G. Sauro/The New York Times; 106: Publiphoto/Strickstein/Houston Post/

Sygma; 107: Benardon/SIPA; 108 top: Canapress; bottom: Paula Penno/Canada Wide; 109 top: Publiphoto/T. Campion/ Sygma; bottom: Sven Simon; 110: Publiphoto/A. Nogues/Sygma; 111 top: Publiphoto/Jason Bleibtreu/Sygma; bottom: Publiphoto/Matsumoto/Sygma; 112–113: Robert Nicholas/Blackstar; 113: Peter Cutler/Canada Wide; 114 left: Pono Presse Int./Visages/Michael Montfort; right: Publiphoto/A. Tannenbaum/Sygma; 115: Pono Presse Int./Gamma/Ron Levy; 116 top left: Eddie Sanderson/Sygma; top right: Bill Smith/Canapress; bottom: Copyright © by Universal Pictures, a Division of Universal City Studios, Inc. Courtesy of MCA Publishing Rights, a Division of MCA Inc.; 17: Steve Schapiro/Sygma; 118: Publiphoto/J.L. Atlan/Sygma; 119 top: Pono Presse Int./ Contact/Louie Psihoyas; bottom: Canapress/Robert Giroux; 120: Brian Willer; 121: UPI/Bettman Newsphotos; 122: Pono Presse Int./Retna Ltd./Larry Busacca; 123 left: Carol Halebian/Gamma-Liaison; right: Chris Volker/Gamma-Liaison; 124: Canapress; 125 top: Brian Willer; bottom: Dennis Hamilton/Gamma-Liaison; 126 left: Pono Presse Int./Gamma/Senet; right: Patrick Harbron; 127: Brian Willer, 128 top left: The Globe and Mail, Toronto; top right: Annick Press; 128 bottom left: Curtis Lantinga; bottom right: Miriam Berkley; 129 top left: Publiphoto/Lionel Derimais/ Sygma; top right: Brian Willer; bottom left: D. Fineman/Sygma; 130 and 131 top left: Brian Willer; 131 top right: Publiphoto/ Ledru/Sygma; bottom: Publiphoto/Ricki Rosen/Picture Group; 132–33 and 134: Patrick Harbron; 135 top: Ken Regan/Camera 5; bottom: Geoffrey Croft/Outline; 136 top: David Redfern/Retna Ltd.; bottom: Patrick Harbron; 137: Brian Willer; 138 top left: Robert Matheu/Retna Ltd.; 138 top right: Brian Willer; bottom: Canapress/ Brian Arts; 139 top: Neal Preston; bottom: Mark Lebon/Retna Ltd.; 140 top: Publiphoto/Matthew Rolston/Outline; bottom: The National Ballet of Canada; 141: Lorraine C. Parow; 142: © Martha Swope 1988; 143: Publiphoto/T. Westenberger/Sygma; 144 top: Necessary Angel Theatre; bottom: Brian Willer; 145 top: A Necessary Angel; bottom: Vancouver East Cultural Centre; 146 top: Publiphoto/Sygma; bottom: Globe Photos; 147 and 148 top: United Artists; 148 middle: Canapress/Bill Becker; bottom: Mantle Clinic II, Ltd.; 149 top: Metro-

Goldwyn-Mayer Pictures, Inc.; **middle**: Warner Bros.; **bottom**: Alliance Releasing; **150 top**: Buena Vista Distribution Co. Inc.; **bottom**: Publiphoto/Alain Dejean/Sygma; **151 and 152 top and bottom**: Paramount Pictures Corp.; **153 top**: Copyright © by Universal Pictures, a Division of Universal City Studios, Inc. Courtesy of MCA Publishing Rights, a Division of MCA Inc.; **153 bottom**: Columbia Pictures; **154 left**: Pono Presse Int./Gamma/G. Gorman; **154 right**: Lucasfilm Ltd.; **155**: Publiphoto/Nancy Ellison/Sygma; **156 left**: United Artists Corporation; **156 right**: Orion Pictures Corporation; **157 top left**: Paramount Pictures Corporation; **157 top right**: Publiphoto/Sygma; **157 bottom**: Paramount Pictures Corporation; **158 top**: Pono Presse Int./Shooting Star/Eddie Sanderson; **158 bottom**: Michaelin McDermott/image courtesy of Kevin Sullivan Films Inc.; **159**: Publiphoto/Tony Cosya/Outline; **160 top**: Canada Wide; **160 bottom**: Janet Webb/Playing With Time; **161 top left**: Pono Presse Int./Shooting Star/G. Trindl; **161 bottom left**: Pono Presse Int./Contact Press Image/Annie Leibovitz; **161 top right**: Canada-Wide; **161 bottom right**: Publiphoto/George Lange/Outline; **162 and 163**: SCTV; **164 top left**: Publiphoto/Sygma; **164 top right**: Brian Willer; **164 bottom left**: Publiphoto/Christopher Little/Outline; **164 bottom right**: Publiphoto/Bertrand Carriere; **165**: Brian Willer; **166 top**: Harold Rosenberg; **bottom left**: courtesy Mary Boone Gallery; **bottom right**: Publiphoto/Leonard Andres Collection/Sygma; **167**: Ron Watts/First Light; **168**: Publiphoto/Villers/Ramsay/Sygma; **169 top**: Brian Willer; **middle**: Rick Eglinton; **bottom**: Brian Willer; **170–71**: Publiphoto/B. Annebicque/Sygma; **172**: Mark O'Neill/Canada Wide; **173 and 174 top**: Brian Willer; **174 bottom**: Publiphoto/Sygma; **175**: Sygma; **176**: Brian Willer; **177**: Canapress; **178**: NASA/courtesy of Spar Aerospace; **179**: R. Perez/Sygma; **180**: Keith Meyers/The New York Times; **181 top**: Bob Rearick/courtesy Loma Linda University Medical Center; **bottom**: Pono Presse Int./Gamma-Liaison/Ravell Call; **182**: courtesy Pat Morrow/First Light; **183**: Brian Willer; **184**: courtesy Professor Owen Beattie/University of Alberta; **185 top**: Rick Friedman/Blackstar; **bottom**: courtesy Ex Terra Foundation; **186**: Brian Willer; **187**: Publiphoto/Ted - Thai/Sygma; **188 top**: Canapress; **188 bottom**: Canapress/Ron Poling; **189 top**: Pono Presse Int./Gamma/

Mitsuhiro Wada; **bottom**: Lincoln Potter/Gamma-Liaison; **190**: Publiphoto/Sygma; **191**: Peter Morgan/Picture Group; **192 top left**: Andrew Sacks; **bottom left**: Brian Willer; **top right**: Brian Condron/Financial Post; **bottom right**: Wardair; **193**: Tom Hollyman; **194**: Peter Sibbald; **195 top left**: Campeau Corporation; **top right**: courtesy McCain Foods Ltd.; **bottom**: Douglas Sinclair; **196 top left**: Press Association Photo Library; **top right**: Canapress; **bottom**: Shirley Black; **197 top**: Brian Willer; **bottom**: The Financial Times of London; **198**: Brian Willer; **199**: Eric Hayes/Miller Comstock; **200 left**: Deborah MacNeill; **200–201**: Ruth Reyno; **202–203**: Ken Straiton/Miller Comstock; **204**: Brian Willer; **205 top**: Randy Moore/Windsor Star; **bottom**: Pono Presse Int./Rex Features; **206 top**: Stan Behal/Canada Wide; **bottom**: Fred Thornhill/Canada Wide; **207**: Ottmar Bierwagen; **208 top left**: Canada Wide; **bottom left**: George Rose/Allsport USA; **top right**: Canapress/Shaney Komulainen; **bottom right**: Canada Wide; **209**: Allsport USA; **210**: Chris Speedie; **211**: Publiphoto/E. Adams/Sygma; **212 top**: Canapress; **bottom**: Publiphoto/Peter Marlow/Sygma; **213 top**: UPI/Bettman Newsphotos; **middle**: Canapress/Mike Blake; **bottom**: Canada Wide; **214**: Publiphoto/T. Campion/Sygma; **215 top**: Publiphoto/E. Preau/Sygma; **bottom**: Publiphoto/Tom Buchanam/Sygma; **216 top**: Canada Wide; **bottom**: Publiphoto/S. Franklin/Sygma; **217 top left and top right**: UPI/Bettman Newsphotos; **bottom**: Publiphoto/D. Auclair; **218**: Stan Behal/Canada Wide; **219**: Canapress; **220**: Publiphoto/G. Rancinan/Sygma; **220–21**: Pono Presse Int./Contact Press Images/David Burnett; **222**: Brian Willer; **223 top**: Ian Tomlinson; **bottom**: Ottmar Bierwagen; **224**: Paul Latour/Ottawa Citizen; **225 left**: Geig Reekie/Canada Wide; **right**: Publiphoto/Seve Finn/Alpha; **226 and 227 top and bottom**: Ottmar Bierwagen; **228**: Duomo/Paul J. Sutton; **229**: Canapress; **230**: Canada Wide; **231**: Brian Willer; **232**: Duomo/Steven E. Sutton; **233**: Canapress; **234 top**: Brian Willer; **bottom**: Theo Westenberger/Sygma; **235**: Ken Regan/Camera 5; **236**: Publiphoto/George Lange/Outline, **237 top**: courtesy Kera, Dallas/Fort Worth/Denton; **bottom**: courtesy Workman Publications; **238**: Miller Comstock; **239 top**: Lorraine C. Parow; **bottom**: Brian Willer; **240**: Steve Schapiro/Sygma; **241**: Publiphoto/G. Zimbel; **242 left**: Alain Masson; **right**: Brian

Willer; **243**: Zefa U.K./Miller Comstock; **244**: Brian Willer; **245**: Alain Masson; **246**: Brian Willer; **247**: Publiphoto/Bertrand Carriere; **248 and 249**: Brian Willer; **250**: City Syndication; **251**: Publiphoto/Stuart Nicol/Alpha; **252 top**: UPI/Bettman Newsphotos; **bottom**: Canada Wide; **253 top left**: Pono Presse Int./Rex Features/Peter Brooker; **top right**: Canapress; **bottom**: Canapress/Ryan Remiorz; **254**: Canapress; **255**: Pono Presse Int./Gamma/De Keerle-Parker; **256 top left**: Pono Presse Int./Images; **bottom left**: Jeff Slocomb/Outline Press; **top right**: Brian Quigley/Outline Press; **bottom right**: Pono Press Int./Agence Angeli; **257**: Canapress/Dave Buston; **258**: Publiphoto/Trapper/Sygma; **259**: Pono Presse Int./Visages/Herb Ritts; **260 top**: Canapress; **middle**: Publiphoto/Richard Corkery/LGI Photo Agency; **bottom**: Pono Presse Int./Gamma; **261 top**: Pono Presse Int.; **bottom**: Canapress/John Major; **262**: Publiphoto/J.L. Atlan/Sygma; **263**: Tim Graham/Sygma; **264**: Brian Willer; **264–65**: Canada Wide; **266**: Brian Willer; **267**: Christopher Morris/Blackstar; **268**: Jack Chiang/Kingston Whig Standard; **269**: Mike Blake/Reuters/Bettman Newsphotos; **270–71**: Douglas Sinclair; **272 top**: Universal Studio; **bottom**: Sven Simon Bonn; **273 left**: © 1977 Nancy Crampton; **center**: Sven Simon Bonn; **right**: Maclean's Photo Library; **274 left**: Maclean's Photo Library; **right**: CBC Picture Service; **275**: Paul Orenstein; **276 top left**: Mike Kesterton; **top middle**: Reuters/Bettmann Newsphotos; **middle**: Sven Simon Bonn; **bottom**: Chapman Collection/Pono Presse; **top right**: Maclean's Photo Library; **277**: Wide World Photo; **278**: Brian Willer; **282 top**: Universal Pictures; **bottom**: Sven Simon; **283 left**: Nancy Crampton; **middle**: Seven Simon; **right**: John McGreevy Productions; **284 top left**: CBC Picture Service; **bottom left**: Reuters/ Bettman Newsphotos; **middle**: Paul Orenstein; **right**: Mike Kesterton; **285 middle**: Pono Presse; **right**: Sven Simon; **286 left**: Brian Willer; **right**: Pono Presse; **jacket top left**: Keystone Canada

Every reasonable effort has been made to ascertain the ownership of photographs used in this book. Information would be welcomed that would enable the publisher to rectify any error.